Archaeological incidents and accidents

David Frankel

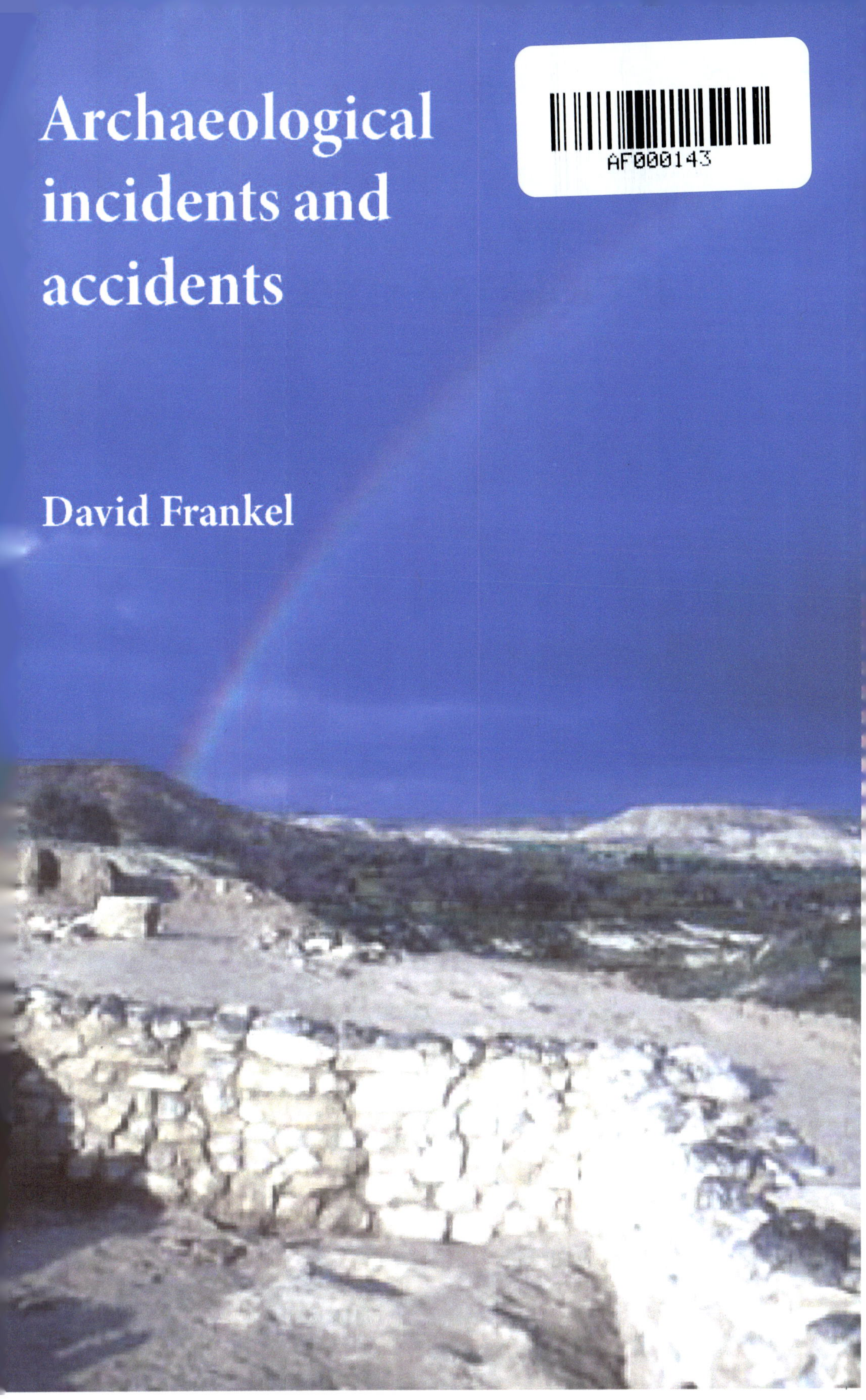

ARCHAEOLOGICAL INCIDENTS AND ACCIDENTS

David Frankel

Archaeological Incidents and Accidents

Melbourne 2025

Copyright © 2025 by David Frankel
d.frankel@latrobe.edu.au

All rights reserved.

No part of this publication may be reproduced, distributed, or transmitted in any form or by any means, including photocopying, recording, or other electronic or mechanical methods, without the prior written permission of the author.

 A catalogue record for this book is available from the National Library of Australia

ISBN 978 0 6456343 9 6

FOR LENA

Contents

Contents		v
About this book		vii
Where in the world?		ix
1	The truth of the matter	1
2	No Sleeping Beauty, this	3
3	Spirits of times past	9
4	Mary-Ann and the seafarer	13
5	A Spirit Board	19
6	An embarrassment of bronze	23
7	Finding Marki	29
8	Observing crafty women	39
9	Time and change	45
10	From one stone tool	55
11	Bull in a china shop	65
12	A mild obsession	73
13	You pays your money	79
14	Lime, chemistry and style	83
15	Not Elizabeth's boot-scraper	91

Contents

16	Obsolescence	95
17	A menagerie	99
18	Water monkeys and wine	103
19	Significance	109
20	By the numbers	115
21	Recycling Sotira	119
22	Questioning mounds	125
23	Strike me pink	131
24	Logistics	133
25	To see oursels	139
26	Development	141
27	What you see is what you get	145
28	Hunting a solution	149
29	Back stories	155
30	Not an afterthought	163
Read more about it		165
The illustrations: notes and credits		175

About this book

It must have been in 2000. I'd given a public lecture in Nicosia the day before and was now at one by the eminent British Classical scholar, Sir John Boardman. Afterwards, a sophisticated, well-educated, well-travelled Cypriot couple came up to me. 'Thank you for yesterday's interesting talk' they said, 'we really enjoyed it and could follow everything so easily. But,' they went on, 'this evening's lecture by Sir Boardman was really something special. Such language, such a high level of English. Just what you'd expect from a famous Professor from Oxford. It was wonderful to hear it, although, of course, we couldn't understand half of what he said — we'd have been disappointed if we had'.

So, avoid disappointment and set your expectations of erudition a bit lower. There'll be little formality in this personal, idiosyncratic look at an odd selection of memories, events, old things and the stories I have told about them: small histories rather than Big History. But then, of course, the past was inhabited by everyday people leading everyday lives.

Archaeological projects, like other research, ought to begin with a clear design. This one doesn't. But it isn't really a piece of research, although it is still one of discovery — discovery of ancient worlds, of some ways in which this can be done, of some half forgotten memories which, as it turns out, expose some of the accidents and incidents that create or redirect opportunities to explore past worlds. These stories are in a somewhat random order, sometimes cycling back to related themes while a few sites and people pop up every now and then. Some of these tales are longer, others shorter and a few taller, although most are more-or-less true.

I have been very lucky in many ways, lucky to have found and been able to pursue a life in the archaeological world and to develop some of the many practical skills this involves, in the field, library, laboratory and at the writing-desk. I have had the

About this book

privilege of being allowed to excavate sites of different kinds in different places, and to respond to the continual challenges they throw up, some of which are presented here.

Lena, who has lived though my obsessions with archaeology since we met in Arad in January 1968, pushed me to write something of them. None of this would ever have been possible without her forbearance and support over many decades.

Many others, too, can take some credit, although no responsibility: friends and family who encouraged this little book; many colleagues who shared their expertise and joined me on some of these voyages of discovery, especially Jenny Webb, Rudy Frank, Caroline Bird, Christine Eslick and the late Ron Vanderwal; innumerable students who happily contributed so much hard work and made my research physically and financially possible; First Nations people whose heritage I have been privileged to explore, particulary those who have commented on some of these stories; friends in Cyprus, especially those in the Department of Antiquities, the University of Cyprus and the Cyprus American Archaeological Research Institute; La Trobe University and the Australian Research Council, the providers of resources and funding for many projects.

Where in the world?

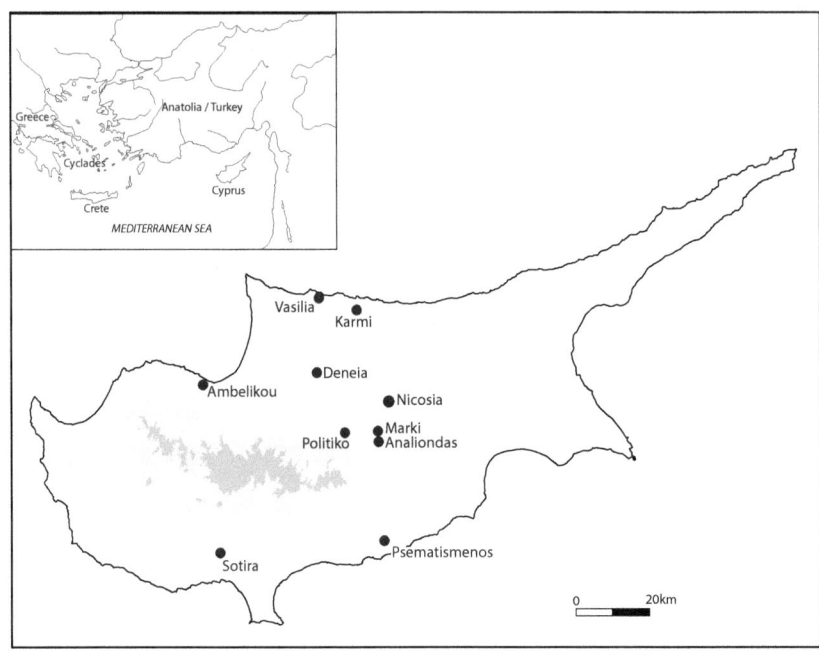

Where in the world?

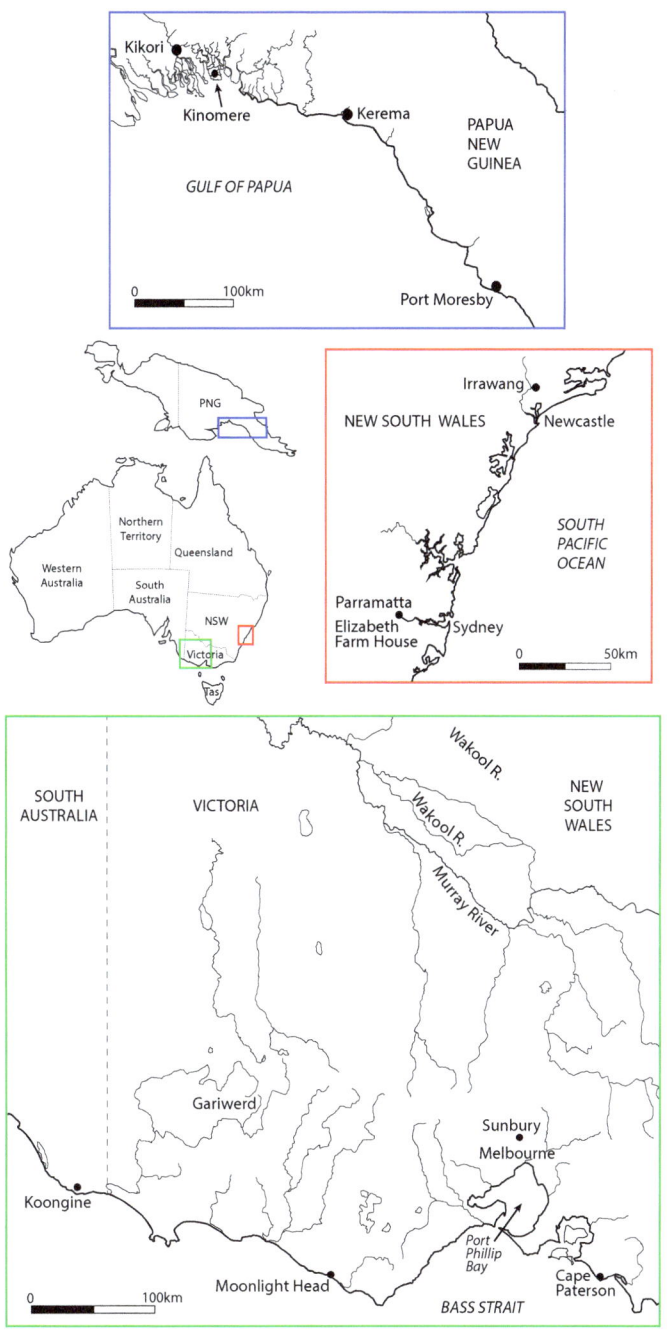

x

1
The truth of the matter

One of the first things I had to learn when I began at the British Museum was how much faith people had in the information on display. Labels had to be accurate and true. When I inserted some up-to-date theory into a text I was told in no uncertain terms not to do so: 'let us wait until it is well established' even though the well-worn text-book versions were clearly now wrong. The newer one could only be used once it was all-but-superseded as it would inevitably be.

This authority of the printed labels was often brought home to me when I proudly showed friends and relations around the displays I'd helped to set up. When I explained the context or identified some object, they would peer closely at the printed descriptions to check if I was right — even though they knew I had written them.

But sometimes even British Museum labels can mislead.

Early one morning I was walking with my Keeper. Not that he was looking after me — Edmond Sollberger, an eminent scholar, was the Keeper of the Department of Western Asiatic Antiquities at the British Museum, and I was a humble Research Assistant, ranking below him, the Deputy Keeper and the Assistant Keepers in the Museum hierarchy. I can't remember what he was saying as we passed impressive sculptures from the palaces of the ancient Assyrian kings. Then he

1. The truth of the matter

suddenly stopped in front of one of the less imposing ones, a four-sided white limestone monument — the so-called White Obelisk, excavated in 1853 from the millennia-old ruins of Nineveh.

I'd never paid much attention to it. The nearby Black Obelisk was both better preserved and always attracted more interest. But Edmond Sollberger had discussed the White Obelisk a few years before, arguing that it recorded and glorified the activities of King Ashurnasirpal I, and not his later namesake Ashurnasirpal II, as others believed. 'Look!' he said, pointing at the label near the base: it was one of those old labels, hand-lettered in white paint on glass, dating from some forgotten time in the Museum's long history. Here, clearly written, was 'Ashurnasirpal II' — the wrong king! He was puzzled, for he had himself noted that the monument's label identified it as from the time of Ashurnasirpal I in his publication. We walked around the obelisk and looked at the other side. There a second, similar ancient label clearly had the opposite opinion: this one, indeed, read 'Ashurnasirpal I'. For a century or more this difference had gone unnoticed.

Not long before this took place, Julian Reade, who taught me what little I know about Assyrian sculpture, had made a very strong case for the later king in a paper published the year we both joined the Department of Western Asiatic Antiquities. Although an established specialist on Assyrian archaeology, he, too, was a lowly Research Assistant.

Guess whose opinion was followed when the conflicting labels were reconciled?

2
No sleeping Beauty, this

My old mentor, the late Paul Åström, spoke of his site as a Sleeping Beauty, awoken to life by the kiss of the prince-as-archaeologist. Other sites might be frogs. Or have different personalities. Some are compliant, happy to be transformed by the touch of the excavator; others remain wild, refusing to play by our rules. One such site is Deneia. Of course no excavation goes quite as expected: tools and the weather may break; students or the site won't always behave; or no-one can find a necessary piece of string. But at Deneia our best laid schemes went seriously awry, for it cheated by enlisting unexpected allies.

Extensive Bronze Age cemeteries around the small central Cypriot village of Deneia were long famous, or at least well known, to two groups of people: a small handful of Cypriot archaeologists and generations of tomb-looters: village farmers whose distant ancestors had bequeathed them the antiquities they could mine to supplement their incomes. Everyone in the village knew of the tombs — how could they not, for the surrounding limestone plateau was pock-marked with innumerable holes and hollows, the opened entrance shafts leading down to underground burial chambers, playgrounds for local lads and convenient

2. No Sleeping Beauty, this

dumps for household refuse — anything from broken fridges to disposable nappies.

Every now and then a few archaeologists gingerly approached these cemeteries — the occasional rescue excavation or scavenging fragments discarded by looters beside the tomb entrances. But all were daunted by their sheer size and inhibited by their own attitudes. Tombs have always attracted excavators' interest, targeted for their rich yield of grave-goods. But any, like those at Deneia, which had already worked over by looters were regarded as of little use, depleted of many items and whatever residue left broken and incomplete. Intact, untouched tombs, with burials in place, accompanied by their full complement of objects, were seen as the ideal of understanding funerary customs and to collect sets of pots suited to traditional description and study.

Our aim was different and more ambitious, fondly imagining we were up to the challenge of taking on the whole sprawling complex rather than focussing on the individual tomb or artefact. We felt that neat, complete tomb-groups were not necessary, and that the despised looted tombs still retained massive quantities of broken fragments. Just the sort of thing we were accustomed to from excavating at settlements. These could provide just as much information as complete items — if only we asked the right questions.

Like others, we'd marvelled at the scale of Deneia and done our share to document the old collections in Oxford and in Sydney. So we knew the site and its potential and had the skills to tame it, although that might take several years. We designed a long-term project: a first phase of documenting all the visible tomb-shafts, valuable in itself and to serve as the basis for an appropriate strategy to extract samples of pottery from selected tombs. The key word was sampling: collecting a sample of material from a sample of tombs.

2. No Sleeping Beauty, this

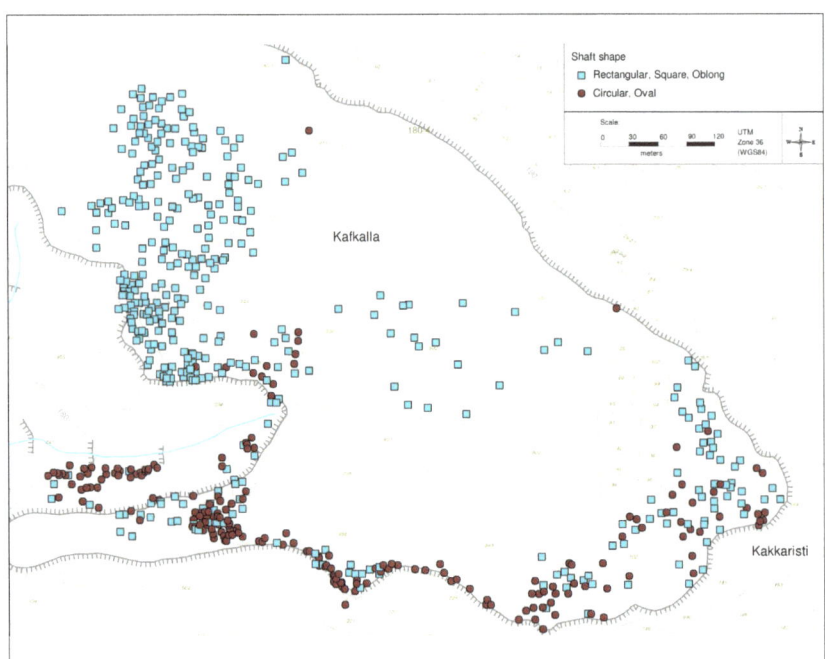

2. No Sleeping Beauty, this

The first phase went well as we happily trudged across the plateaus and their slopes, finding, and describing the hundreds of open tomb entrances and we hadn't even seen one snake. We then plotted their location, a task made possible using the newly available magic of GPS. Nowadays it would probably be possible to use a mobile phone, and we'd certainly enjoy playing with drones; but then, even only a couple of decades ago, these were not even dreamt of. The GPS we were so proud of was big, bulky and heavy. Rudy strapped it on his back and heroically tramped from one yellow-flagged tomb to another, all through the long hot days. So at the end of the field season we had as good a map of the whole area as was possible, with sufficient details to tell a good story of differences in tomb size and shape to provide the basis for Phase Two.

We also spent time finding accommodation for students in the

village and to arrange to rent a very large shed — appropriately once a local pottery workshop. We had never had such a spacious place to work, ample room to spread out and deal with the many sherds we expected to collect in Phase Two. Almost all our team came from Australia — eager students willing to pay the airfare to work with us for two long months over the long Australian summer break — winter, of course, in Cyprus. So there we were, in November 2004, all three dozen of us, with our mountain of tools and equipment, lodged and sorted in several houses and in our big work shed. All the domestic logistics organised, perhaps the hardest part of any project.

At first all went well. Neat square or circular shafts went down a metre or more though the limestone capping, with smaller holes leading into the oval underground chambers: in some cases extensive caverns opened up below the limestone, with access from several shafts. Their faces masked against the dust, students crawled down into the dim holes of several tombs, laid out areas to excavate and hauled the pottery-rich spoil to the surface where artefacts and bones could be carefully picked out of the sieves. Minor discomforts like flea bites were happily ignored, and the sherds piled up in the workroom: all to be washed, sorted, counted. The search for joining pieces which might be mended into more complete vessels began, and all the more interesting items drawn and photographed.

But then it all changed. Within two or three days, first one or two, then more and more of the students became sick, many quite seriously ill. We'd never seen anything like it. Not the usual minor complaints but something far worse. Doctors were hard to find, but eventually we had a possible diagnosis: *murine typhus!*

2. No Sleeping Beauty, this

We didn't know what that was, but it sounded bad. It was, as we learnt, endemic in many country areas, carried by rodents and transmitted to people by fleas — those little bites were not as trivial as we'd assumed. We sought help from everyone we knew or could find, from the Australian High Commissioner to the United Nations doctors. Diagnosis and appropriate antibiotics cured everyone.

But clearly we could no longer work in such unhealthy tombs. Our entire project had to be abandoned. Cypriot colleagues provided alternative fieldwork for those of our students who were not needed to process the 21,936 sherds that had been recovered in those few days. That kept us busy enough, once we'd calmed down our anxious students, reassured their nervous parents back home, the University appeased, concerned as it was about Health and Safety — and possible insurance claims.

Our colleagues at the Cyprus Museum and university had never even heard of the disease: they were both horrified and upset by this attack: it was, after all, quite against their cultural ethic of *philoxenia*.

The cemeteries at Deneia had a different view of hospitality to strangers!

3
Spirits of times past

The Men's House was far from comfortable. Newly built and still unfinished, its floor of uneven and unsteady wooden slats raised high above the ground on narrow stilts. The whole space was open and bare: there were none of the internal divisions, hung with spirit-boards and skull-racks, seen in all their frightening and exotic detail in the images captured by Frank Hurley when he visited Kinomere Village in 1921. Then, cathedral-like Men's Houses dominated the village: forbidden to women, they were the centres of mystery, of ancestral histories and social control, where ceremonies were planned and objects of power and awe prepared and secreted, awaiting revelation in sacred performances.

That world was undermined and its symbols later destroyed when missionaries invaded the Papuan Gulf. In Kinomere Village the old Men's Houses also burned. The new House we called home for a few weeks in 1981 was only a pale imitation.

Ron, Kym and I were there to explore the older history of the village, deep in the low tidal delta of the Kikori River in the Papuan Gulf: a land of mud and water, where green tunnels of nipa palm fronds arch over the maze of channels. At low tide Kinomere Village is surrounded by deep, sticky mud. At high tide the water rises between the roots of the mangroves and flows beside the

3. Spirits of times past

jetties and projecting stilt-houses which surround its central open space. Here low hummocks are covered by lush green vegetation. But it is not natural ground. The dry land is an artificial creation of spongy accumulations of vegetation, waste products of repairs and manufactures: old shelters, fences and canoes. And, mixed in with this is a share of domestic refuse: animal bones, shells, tools and ornaments. In the olden days, the '*time bilong bepo*', this included pottery, traded into the Gulf from areas near Port Moresby, 400 kilometres to the east. That was what we were looking for – things we could use to trace the history of this amazing long-distance trade, where fleets of Motu sailors shipped thousands of pots to exchange for tons of sago.

Our aim was clear. We were there to excavate the artificial mounds in the village, to collect samples of pottery and take them home to Melbourne for documentation and analysis: clear, rational, formal science.

The villagers were happy to have us there: indeed news of our planned visit prompted them to start work on the new Men's House – for where else could they accommodate us? What we

3. Spirits of times past

wanted to do was a bit harder to understand. Strange white men often did strange things, that was taken for granted. Dig a hole in the centre of the village? Why not, so long as ancestral and other spiritual forces could be appeased. A sack of rice would do this, providing a feast for people of this and other worlds – the Australian Research Council would later see this line item in our budget as 'local excavation permit'.

So we began to dig, through the upper organic to lower more compact soils. Here and there were remnants of upright piles, once the props for long-vanished buildings, perhaps one of the Men's Houses of the 1920s. All-too-soon, but not unexpectedly, we reached water. But we found sufficient fragments of pottery. Success!

Meanwhile we provided amusement for the children, who happily helped, while the old men watched. And thought. Distant memories of World War II action suggested a gun emplacement; or perhaps we were digging a well, or maybe installing a water-tank. By the end of our

3. Spirits of times past

visit they'd worked it out. We must be ancestral beings, returning to the village to look for something we'd lost when we lived there in the 'time bilong bipo'. And certainly I, for one, was clearly a ghost: tall, thin, strangely translucently white.

This they somewhat hesitantly explained to us. Not that we would be upset to be identified, but rather because they had another difficulty. They were all devout Christians — Seventh-Day Adventists, through whatever accident had imposed missionaries of that sect on them. So they didn't really believe in ancestral spirits. But still, that is what we must clearly be, missionaries or no missionaries.

Naturally we said we were not. Ghosts?... huh! And at the time saw this as another example of a common reaction, often reported by anthropologists. Not till later did I stop to think again. The old men thought I was a ghost — *how do I know I was not?*

What other reason would I have for going to such lengths to visit this remote and uncomfortable place, and to dig just *there,* precisely *there.* And, having found whatever it was I needed to find, or resolved whatever conflict or trauma needed closure, I had no need or desire to return again. Was this — or many another — archaeological project just a cover story, a convenient, socially and intellectually acceptable (if culturally arrogant) means to find resolution or repair loss through excavation and discovery?

4
Mary-Ann and the Seafarer

Archaeology's worst — and worst-kept — secret is that many, maybe even most, excavators fail to publish adequate (or indeed any) reports on what they did and what they found. There are many excuses for this moral failure, ranging from the psychological to the commercial, but few are acceptable. But we can excuse James Stewart, the Edwin Cuthbert Hall Professor of Archaeology at the University of Sydney. He was seriously ill while excavating two Bronze Age cemeteries at Karmi in Cyprus; less than a year later  he was dead. He did manage to put together one study of what he regarded as 'the most important discovery since the 1890's, since it is so definite and the repercussions so wide spread'. His paper on 'The Tomb of the Seafarer at Karmi' was published posthumously in 1962. It would be fifty years before Jenny Webb, Kathryn Eriksson and I completed the full report on the Palealona and Lapatsa cemeteries.

In a hangover from the recently ended colonial system Stewart was able to export almost all the finds from Cyprus to Australia, 72 crates of them. A decade later, as a student, I used on occasion to drive out to Professor Basil Hennessy's property on the outskirts of Sydney and then travel on with him for another hour up to Wentworth Falls in the Blue Mountains. There, James Stewart's

4. Mary-Ann and the Seafarer

widow, Eve, lived with the masses of pottery from these and other sites, guarding and continuing to work on his massive *Corpus of Cypriot Antiquities*, a monument, worthy of Gormenghast, to a personal vision of archaeological analysis. Once refreshed from our journey we would visit the innumerable sherds that lay spread across large tables, making desultory attempts to match and mend fragments of some vessels. After a substantial Sunday roast lunch we would do a little more before it was time to head home. It is no wonder that little progress was made: it would be many years before Kathryn Eriksson brought order to the chaos. I was still too naïve to realise this when I first met Vassos Karageorghis, the formidable Director of the Department of Antiquities in Nicosia. Basil had charged me with a message to him: 'Tell Vassos that the publication of Stewart's excavations will soon be completed'. Vassos simply laughed – he knew far better!

When we finally began to prepare the comprehensive report our task was made all the harder because some tomb-groups had been dispersed across the globe. Most are now in Sydney, finally brought into the collections of the Nicholson (now Chau Chak Wing) Museum, but others went elsewhere in Australia, and to America, New Zealand and Sweden. This was another vestige of past practices, where museums provided funds in return for a share of the finds – a practice which encouraged, at least in the case of Cyprus, excavations of tombs rich in complete vessels, and a corresponding avoidance of settlement sites, with only broken fragments to show. Inevitably, during this piecemeal distribution, some things went missing: lost, or stolen or strayed. The fieldnotes, too, could no longer be found, with conflicting and acrimonious versions of how, when and where they disappeared.

But fortunately photographs of the excavations and Eve Stewart's meticulous, detailed, large-scale plans of the tombs and the location of the things within them still survived.

Back in 1961 Stewart was at first grumpily disappointed

with the tombs at Karmi. Many of the underground tomb chambers had collapsed or been badly damaged, and the grave-goods were unimpressive. But early frustration was replaced by greater enthusiasm, especially with the discovery of 'Mary-Ann' and the Seafarer.

Hidden in a corner of the Cyprus Museum is the neglected cast of a roughly shaped human figure. Standing about 1.5m tall it is a copy of the only large prehistoric carving known from the island. The original still stands against the right-hand side wall of the sloping passage leading down to the entrance to Palaealona Tomb 6. It is not well preserved, and was perhaps never finely carved, while digging out the earth and stones that filled the passage and cleaning around such an unexpected feature may well have caused some additional damage to the soft limestone. There is therefore room for debate regarding its sex. The excavators saw it as female, and dubbed it 'Mary-Ann' after one of the team – one hopes with her approval.

'Mary-Ann' and other associated carved features were so exceptional that it was decided to build a small hut to protect them

4. Mary-Ann and the Seafarer

now that they were exposed to the weather. This required the clearance of the entrance to the neighbouring Tomb 11, whose main chamber had already been excavated. In doing so two more tomb chambers were discovered. One was looted and was not explored further. But the other was an unusually small chamber hollowed out of the side of the entrance shaft. It was used just the

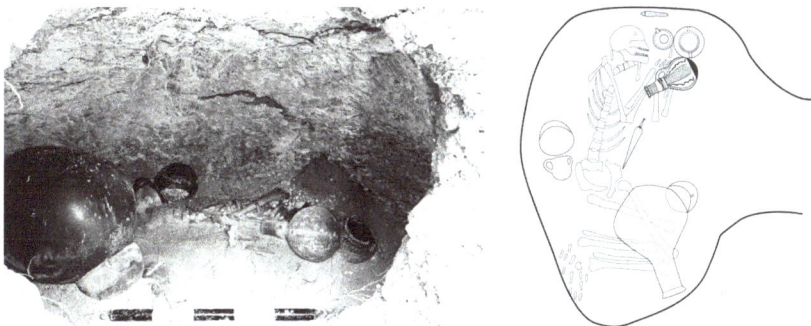

once for a single burial. This is what excited Stewart the most.

It was not the quantity of material, for there were only eight pottery vessels, a copper dagger and a faience bead accompanying the body. But with no possibility of admixture from different times, the pottery showed the burial must have taken place during what we call the Middle Cypriot I Period. And, what made this especially significant ('the most important discovery since the 1890's') was that one of the pottery vessels, a small colourfully

4. Mary-Ann and the Seafarer

decorated cup, was not Cypriot, but came from Crete. Here was a clear connection between the two islands, which also established a helpful link in working out the actual date, for Crete could be tied to other more firmly established chronologies.

Stewart presented the evidence and – in stark contrast to the incomprehensible coded classifications in his *Corpus,* wrote that

'In view of the Kamares cup and the blue faience bead I have called this grave 'The Tomb of the Seafarer' because I believe that the man probably walked down to the sea at Lapithos and took service with one of the vessels trading between Syrian ports and the Aegean and that the two objects are mementos of his travels ... This is perhaps pure fantasy ....'

It would even be tempting to take the 'fantasy' further and see him as a 4,000 year old precursor of Orestes in the 1970s film, shot in Karmi village a decade after Stewart worked there. Returning home from abroad, Orestes' involvement with Eleni (Raquel Welsh – no doubts about her sexual identity!) provides a story of powerful passions and extreme violence in a small village. Her visit to Cyprus excited everyone, including the President, Archbishop Makarios III.

But, unfortunately, thanks to a close examination of the Seafarers' bones by Kirsi Lorentz, we now know that he was about 60 when he died – a relatively old age for the time. He was about 160 cm tall and, not surprisingly, had extensive dental wear because of his age and the high level of grit common in the diet. He also had some severe congenital conditions which affected his spine and lower back and so must have suffered from reduced mobility all through his long life. This would certainly have precluded his taking ship and working as a sailor before returning to his native village in the northern hills of Cyprus.

But how and why he acquired and was buried with the Cretan cup remains a mystery.

17

5
A Spirit Board

It was yet another rainy day in the Long House. Morovi Iuaia sat on the slat floor with his tools beside him: a sharpening file; a knife; several flat, narrow chisels (one made from a screwdriver); and a square blade, perhaps originally from a stanley-knife hafted in a wooden handle and used for scoring and carving outlines. He also had brushes of different widths made from small sticks with the ends beaten and crushed lightly to form bristles. For the next three hours he took me, Ron and Kym through the process of carving and painting a Spirit or Gope Board.

He was an expert at this, producing carvings for sale rather than ceremonial use. Similar long, oval boards are found in many villages in the Gulf Province of Papua New Guinea, varying in style, form and name. While the most obvious common element is a schematic frontal human face, a small circular navel

incorporated into the lower design is often the more significant element, as an entry point for spirits; for such Spirit Boards traditionally provided people a link to their ancestors. Many smaller ones were neither secret nor sacred, but larger, important

5. A Spirit Board

boards were far more potent: they represented, housed or embodied powerful nature spirits. Such more dangerous things were therefore kept in shrines or hidden when not involved in ceremonies

Larger Gope were sometimes incorporated into skull-racks and similar structures, often forming part of the clan divisions within the large Long Houses where they were stored, as seen in Frank Hurley's famous photographs taken in the 1920s. Those impressive Long Houses had been destroyed many years before we visited Kinomere in 1981: the new Long House we lived in was a pale reflection of former grandeur: bare, unfurnished and far from comfortable.

Morovi Iuaia brought with him a piece of light wood salvaged from the side of an old canoe, cut to shape and stained black over a smoky fire. He set to work, his experienced eye and hand creating regular symmetrical designs without the need for any formal measurement. Most work was done with one or other of his chisels, first completing one side and then repeating the process on the other. At all stages the carver worked symmetrically, with completion of aspects of one side immediately followed by those on the opposite side of the board. Throughout the process there was a constant shift in appearance from solid to outlined forms and between light-on-dark and dark-on-light outlines as different

5. A Spirit Board

elements were cut away and gained and lost prominence.

In the early stages, especially in setting out the key central face, the outline of a design or design element was lightly scratched into the darkened surface before scoring it more deeply with a sharp blade and then chiselling out wider grooves, removing the dark surface to expose the light wood below. Later supplementary surrounding designs did not involve any preliminary marking or layout, but just decisive, strong initial cuts with a knife or thin chisel.

5. A Spirit Board

Once the main carving of the face and supplementary geometric designs was completed, time was spent contemplating the board before the final stages. This more delicate work was done carefully, occasionally tentatively, although normally single hard strokes were used to make cuts into the dark surface around and parallel to the cut-away areas and leaving a very narrow border. When the last areas of dark wood were removed all the design stood out as thin, dark, reserved raised lines.

Now colour could be added to the areas of exposed wood. The quality of the red (ochre) and white (lime) paints was of particular concern. 'Too thin! Too pale!' More ochre and lime was mixed in before first the white and then the red paint was applied.

The final, now brightly coloured product was now proudly displayed — ready for use, or, in this case, sale. It did not have the important small, circular navel, deliberately left off as it was a decorative piece, devoid of any power and esoteric significance and suitable for the likes of us, but a reminder of the investment of time and skill in ancient traditional artefacts.

6
An embarrassment of bronze

'You may be interested in this', Charles said, 'and perhaps you have some idea what it is and what to do with it'. He handed me a small, dusty cardboard box as we walked up the stairs from the garage into his house in Cedar Falls.

As soon as I opened it I could guess what the small metal spirals inside it were.

'How did you come to have this?'

'Well, so far as I remember, years ago Stuart gave it to me in Cyprus to bring to America, but, as I heard nothing more from him, I didn't know what to do about it'.

Now I knew that an American colleague, like Charles and me a specialist in Cypriot archaeology, had visited Australia many years earlier. While there he managed to persuade those in charge of the Museum of Antiquities of the University of New England in Armidale to let him drill samples from 17 Cypriot Bronze Age metal items. This was something quite unusual, for museum curators are, as a rule, jealously protective of the things in their care. Once or twice when we met in Cyprus I'd asked Stuart what had happened to the samples and whether he had any results from the analyses he planned. I'd never got a clear answer. Now I knew why! He, too, had lost track of the arrangement and didn't know what had become of his bits and pieces.

I explained all this to Charles. He was happy to be rid of this small embarrassment. After contacting Stuart, who after so long a delay was not so interested in that old

6. An embarrassment of bronze

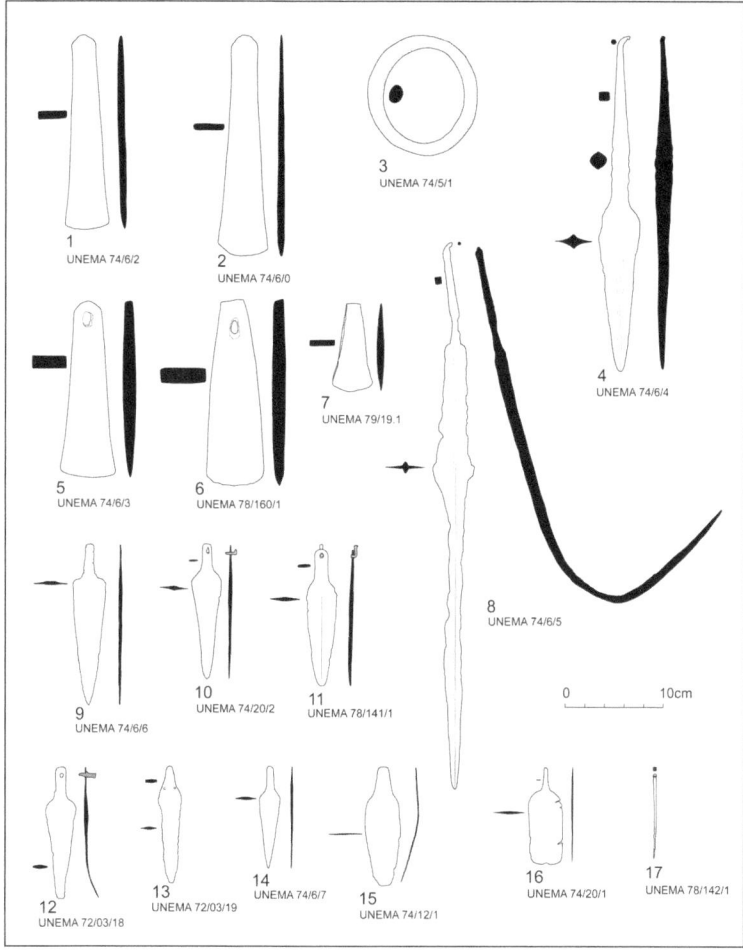

project, the samples came back to Australia. With the Museum's agreement, Stuart generously handed over any rights, and we arranged for the samples to be analysed. Apart from a general belief that it would be best to do something to justify the damage to the objects, several of the items were of particular interest as they came from the very earliest phase of the Cypriot Bronze Age, still something of a mysterious period.

A brief digression. For a century or more we have been saddled with the term 'Bronze Age', adopted and adapted across Europe and beyond. Not that the metal alloy, bronze, was a necessary component: people of many a Bronze Age culture or period made

6. An embarrassment of bronze

no actual bronze but used unalloyed copper. As elsewhere, the Cypriot Bronze Age was further subdivided into Early, Middle and Late, and then each of these sub-divided again and again. These were defined by ever refined pottery types, and everyone understood, more or less, what was what. But then, just when it all seemed neat and tidy, with the Bronze Age beginning with Early Bronze Age IA (or Early Cypriot IA) some pottery was found which didn't fit. If these were earlier than Early Cypriot IA, what should they be called? What name could come before Early Cypriot IA? M*uch debate!* — especially as two strongly opposed opinions emerged. Was this stuff earlier than the earliest known Bronze Age, or was it a regional variation, something James Stewart preferred? Eventually it was easiest to simply name this nuisance after the site where this type of pottery was first found, and so we have the Philia period, phase, facies or regional culture. Incidentally, we can now show from our excavations at Marki that the Philia material is indeed earlier than the conventional Early Cypriot I. For more on this see Story 29.

The metalwork sampled came to the museum in Armidale from James Stewart's excavations and private collection. We have already met him, excavating tombs of the Early and Middle Bronze Age at Karmi. Alongside his formal archaeological work he also bought antiquities — a rather dubious practice, one might think, as it only encouraged further looting of ancient sites. But, as with many moral issues, this is not always so straightforward, for antiquities dealers often had unusual objects for sale. Some of these things have an intrinsic interest, although they don't have the necessary context so essential for understanding the past. Before he excavated at Karmi, Stewart worked at nearby Vasilia. Here the tombs had Philia pottery, and, sealed in one tomb, a cache or hoard of metal items. Unfortunately, others were also busy at the site at the same time; or, really, when the archaeologists were no longer there. Their loot was then for sale in Nicosia. Some things were just like those found by Stewart, and he believed that these looted items all came from Vasilia. What to do? A strict view would be to have nothing to do with any of it, but both James Stewart and the Cypriot Department of Antiquities felt ownership was more important than scruples or the questionable relationships

6. An embarrassment of bronze

that might develop between authorities and dealers. Stewart's purchases of Philia objects ended up in Armidale where they were sampled nearly three decades later.

Enough moral philosophy, and back to the archaeology.

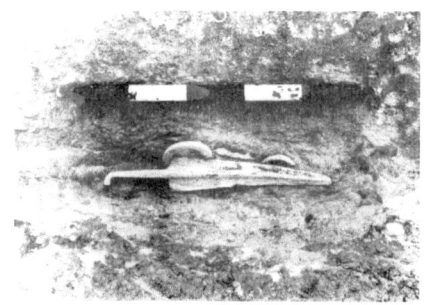

Most of the 17 metal artefacts were from later phases of the Bronze Age, and not so very interesting, as both copper and bronze were known to be regularly used. But the eight pieces from (or, if you want to be pedantic, probably from) Vasilia were of special interest as they were among the earliest metal objects in Cyprus. Metallurgy was one of many crafts and customs introduced to the island at the beginning of the Bronze Age. We can identify innovations in housing, burials, agriculture (such as the use of the

plough), domesticated animals (including cattle) along with new techniques of pottery-making and textile-production. You won't be surprised to know that the cultural and historical processes involved in these introductions has led to much debate. I favour a movement of people to the island, probably from Anatolia (Turkey), others are less inclined to do so. In addition the nature of the interaction between indigenous people (we call them Chalcolithic) and newcomers (our Philia folk) is a rich field for discussion and future research.

What have our analyses to contribute? First of all, compositional analysis showed most of the 17 items were relatively pure copper.

6. An embarrassment of bronze

It may have been the 'Bronze Age' but that doesn't mean everyone always used bronze. But three of the seven Philia items from (strictly speaking, probably from) Vasilia were bronze, with 10% or more tin alloyed with the copper. Now, here is something else you must know: there is no tin to be found in Cyprus. Lots of copper (Cyprus in antiquity was famous for its copper, and some say its very name comes from the Latin for the metal) but no tin. So all the tin was imported, either by itself or already alloyed with copper, perhaps already cast into finished tools. This was probably the case with two of the Philia bronze items which on the basis of their shape are likely to have been made in Anatolia.

Lead Isotope Analysis provides additional information. Some more explanation is needed. Copper also includes tiny, tiny amounts of lead, and lead comes in slightly different forms — different isotopes of the element. Each ore body has characteristic proportions of these isotopes, so if you can measure these it is possible to say where the copper was mined. Such an analysis showed that three of the Philia items were made using Anatolian copper and another three from the Cyclades, far to the west in the Aegean Sea.

So, after all this science, we can see a complex set of relationships between some of our earliest Bronze Age Cypriots and people in Anatolia to the north and the Cyclades to the west. The island was drawn into a web of relationships linking different parts of the eastern Mediterranean. People using copper (or bronze) were travelling between different areas, moving goods, including metals, from one place to another. It is not too far-fetched to see prospectors exploring the island, identifying rich bodies of copper ore, encouraging others to move across the sea. Some came as prospectors and miners, others as farmers, all bringing with them habits, techniques, customs and language which developed into those of the Early and then Middle Bronze Age on the island. We now need to find out more of the impact of all this on the Chalcolithic communities, and how and why their characteristic way of life disappeared – at least from the archaeological record.

7
Finding Marki

'Found anything yet?'

Excavators are well used to this equivalent of the almost obligatory 'caught anything yet?' asked of anyone with a fishing rod. Idle curiosity, perhaps: or the need to show interest but not knowing what else to say. But also reflecting the predominant view that archaeology is about discovery, akin to treasure hunting.

There is no denying the thrill as some special thing reveals itself. Or the pleasure – the satisfaction – when a predicted solution to one of the constant small puzzles thrown up in the field turns out to be correct: a small win in the endless contest between excavator and the site.

But, and repetition makes it no less true, we are – or would like to think we are – finding out rather than just finding. If we knew

7. Finding Marki

the answers there would be no need for the tedious business of digging. But the answers, and the additional questions they raise in turn, may only appear well away from the field or well after that messy business is over.

We worked at Early and Middle Bronze Age Marki for a few months each Cypriot winter year from 1990 to 2000. A modest enough project, involving teams of up to three dozen students. For six days a week most worked with pick and shovel, trowel and brush, bucket and barrow from dawn to dusk; sometimes hot, sometimes wet and sometimes almost freezing. Over all those seasons I probably spent more time in that particular paddock than anyone else had done for several thousand years. Meanwhile Jenny Webb managed her smaller group at home, processing the artefacts harvested each day. The hundreds and thousands of fragments of pottery all needed to be washed, sorted and counted, while several thousands of the more useful bits and pieces had to be documented in obsessive detail, measured, drawn and photographed.

Washing sherds is not much fun: those rostered on to do this could not wait to get back out where the 'real' action was. Anyone feeling a bit unwell, and not up to the demands in the field, took on this milder task instead. That, more often than not, soon cured any minor complaint!

Such a parallel process of excavation and documentation is by no means universal: many projects put far more effort into the excavation, taking advantage of every minute of time available. Then, some time later, a 'study season' would be dedicated to processing the finds. We chose the alternative strategy, and were immensely pleased with ourselves as this meant that at the end of each field season all the finds were thoroughly dealt with, and we didn't have the daunting prospect of one day having to deal with all the accumulated stuff hanging over our heads. Instead we could carry loads of notes, drawings, photographs and computer files home to Melbourne, ready to prepare preliminary reports for the Department of Antiquities and to be worked into our final publication.

These annual preliminary reports were just that: initial descriptions of what we did and found, and how we felt this mattered, perhaps highlighting anything special. And useful, of course, in fulfilling our immediate obligations to the Cypriot authorities, planning the next season and — no small thing — providing justifications for additional research funds. But, such reports are still more about discovery than about understanding. That would come far later, as we learnt more from and about the site as it taught us to read it better.

We, like many an excavator, initially approached the site with a combination of innocence and ignorance. We had two main preconceptions about the structure of Bronze Age villages and their histories, based on limited evidence and sometimes misleading explanations of previous researchers. One was that villages were of short duration, never lasting more than a few generations before people moved to another location. The other was that individual houses were planned in groups (much as a more modern-day terrace), or were constructed close to one another, often sharing party walls. It took time to see things differently.

Time was the key. But it took a while before we really worked out what was going on, simple though it is in retrospect. Look where Peter is drawing what he has just finished excavating. In front of

7. Finding Marki

him are three walls, one above the other, but each offset a little from the one below. He has uncovered three periods of rebuilding: each time the upper courses of mud-brick were demolished, leaving only the lower stone footings, and each time the wall was rebuilt on the same alignment, but just offset a little. There was significant rebuilding, but the common alignment and displacement of the walls tells us that household boundaries were maintained, perhaps something to do with ownership but perhaps more simply the constraints  imposed by neighbouring buildings. In the background there were no earlier walls, only one, built at the same time as the latest of the other three. Something different went on there.

Nearby Delese has found a hearth with a low semicircular plaster surround. It is backed by a low bench running along the base of the stone wall-footing. But notice that these stones do not extend all the way across the room: at the far end is a gap filled with  neatly laid mud-bricks. This was originally a doorway into the room, sealed up when the plaster features were put in place. The next picture expands the story. On the left is Delese's hearth, but on the right you can just make out the remnants of an earlier one, removed when a doorway was broken through the wall behind it when the old door was blocked up. It was a relatively minor renovation, but it cut this small room off from the house of which

7. *Finding Marki*

it was originally a part and connected it to an entirely different one. Imagine the negotiations within the family or between neighbours that must have taken place!

A third area: more of a muddle, but I'm sure you can see the walls built at different times. On the right the latest wall was again built offset from its predecessor, in this case on top of some surviving courses of mud-brick. The same goes for the other, uppermost walls. But at the bottom, beside the older pits are fragments of the earliest building. These date from the time when

33

7. Finding Marki

the village was very new very early in the Bronze Age: the other walls are later, for the place was occupied for about 400 years. Not such a short time!

So, our old preconceptions were wrong: villages lasted a good long while, and the buildings within them had complex histories of building, demolition, rebuilding and renovation of different sorts and at different times.

Disentangling all this was a challenge. We had a mountain of fieldnotes, plans and photographs. Fieldnotes are a funny business: important, basic, but not gospel. Out in the field I'd discuss, advise and oversee work in several areas, in each of which supervisors would manage their fellow students and document what was going on. Not all were as good as Peter and Delese. Sometimes they got things wrong, forgot to write down something essential or misunderstood what I wanted them to say or do. And, remember, I was the only one who had been out there all day, every day, over the hundreds of days of the excavation, had painfully learnt what to look for and appreciate, and could to interpret the notes based on an intimate relationship with site. So I could read the notes as no-one else ever could, and so start to

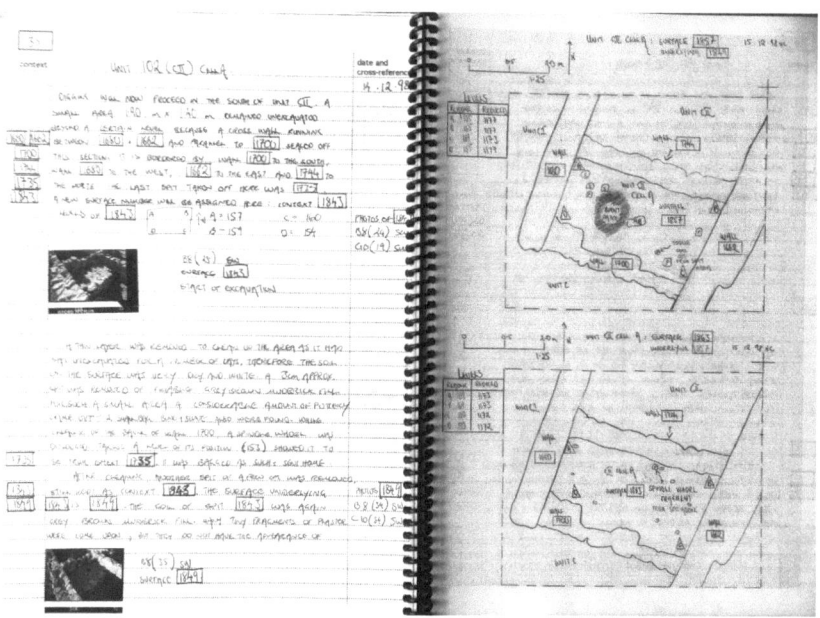

7. Finding Marki

organise a story of developments in each of the dozens of separate excavation units.

Then came the harder task of refining, correcting and integrating these disparate stories. Here the hundreds of 35mm slides I'd taken came into play – it was, of course, before the days of digital photography. Over many days and weeks Jenny and I closely studied each area in turn, projecting the slides in order, following the process of excavation and identifying each feature. As we did this some things not recognised in the field, or misunderstood, or perhaps not seen through some trick of the light, took the opportunity to reveal themselves. Then starting from the bottom we'd work back up to the surface, tracing the sequence of developments – the process repeated until we were happy with the result, drawing up a diagram showing the relationships between all walls and features. Once each area was done, we'd turn to its neighbour, perhaps on the other side of a wall. And then we had to make sure the two adjacent areas told the same story, reviewing, correcting and refining both, adding in the next one, and the next, until gradually everything could be incorporated into one complex sequence. This we divided into ten convenient main phases of building and rebuilding, with more minor, local changes within each.

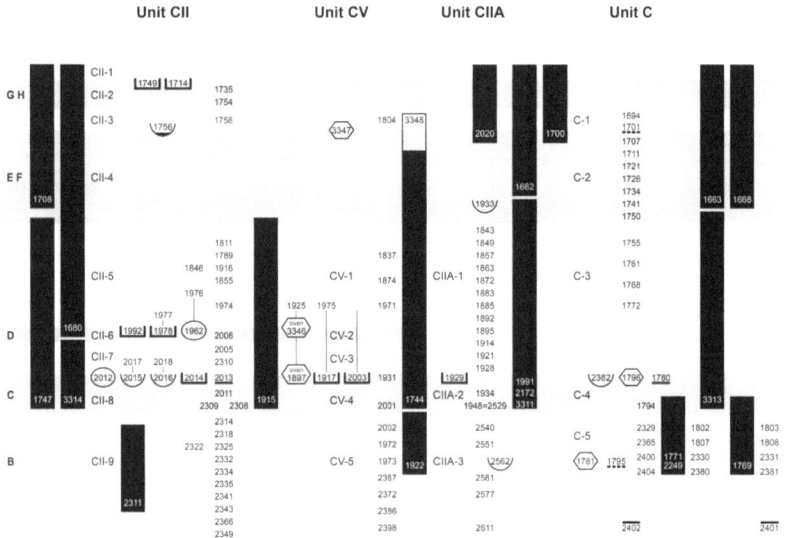

35

7. Finding Marki

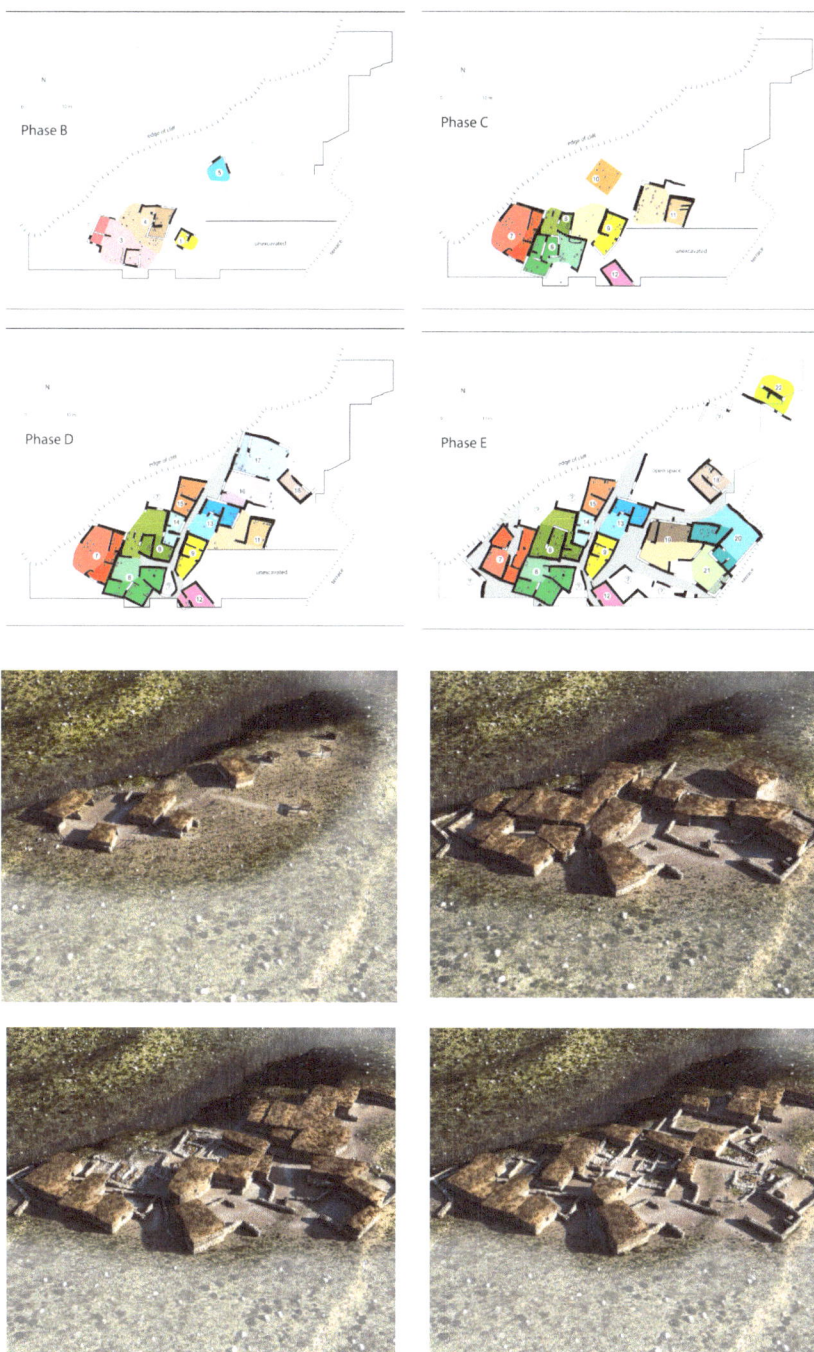

7. Finding Marki

Only now could we draw up plans of these main phases: at last the site began to make sense. We started to see rooms as parts of compounds with open courtyards and interior covered areas, and with laneways and access routes between each as the built-up area became more crowded.

This was our 'eureka' moment. This is when, suddenly, the whole picture fell into place. We had an entirely new understanding of the structure of the village, the history of its individual compounds and their evolving relationships over the generations.

We had, two years after we'd finished ten seasons of excavation, finally found Marki.

8
Observing crafty women

P8422 is an odd-shaped, roughly conical little thing with a central hole through it. It is solid fired clay, weighing in at 54g, so relatively heavy for its size. We found it in the ruins of a house of the Early Bronze Age at Marki in Cyprus and is about 4,000 years old. It is far from unique, there are many similar items, some just broken fragments. These, naturally, were simply tossed aside as useless. But many, like P8422, are complete, still functionally useable. Why were they discarded? Were they lost or forgotten, or perhaps simply set aside as too old or old-fashioned. Or even — who knows? — thrown out with other junk when their owner died. There is plenty of room for idle speculation.

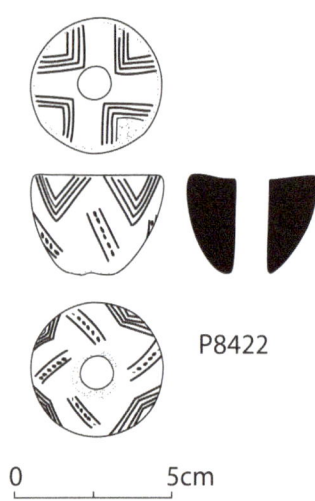

P8422

0   5cm

Its function is no puzzle: it's a spindle-whorl, the weight threaded onto a wooden spindle, where it would provide momentum to its spin as it drew out fibres from the distaff and twisted them into thread. Probably — who is to say different? — a women's tool. This example is neatly decorated with a design incised into the wet clay before it was fired hard. Not all whorls were decorated in this way, but most were, with innumerable variations and combinations of lines, dots and dashes on the broader end and around the sides. Those Bronze

39

8. Observing crafty women

Age women liked their personal, domestic equipment to look and feel good.

Look closely at our whorl. The narrow end is chipped and broken. Why? For generations Cypriot archaeologists illustrated whorls with the broad end down, largely, I suspect, because the orientation didn't seem to matter and it wouldn't fall over when set out for photography or display. But that damaged end told us that this was the wrong way up: the narrow end should be at the bottom — and this, in turn, starts to reveal something about exactly how it was used.

There are two main spinning traditions in the ancient world. In some places women use high-whorl spindles, with the weight placed near the top of the spindle. Elsewhere, the whorls are placed near the bottom, with the yarn neatly collected on the spindle above it. I couldn't use either type, but am told that people growing up in a high-whorl tradition have great difficulty using low-whorl spindles and vice versa. It is a matter of early acquired habitual fine motor skills, such as those which make it almost impossible for Americans to play cricket. The damaged end shows that these whorls were mounted at the bottom of the spindle — more specifically, of a drop spindle. In this tradition the spindle is spun as it is dropped — much like a yo-yo — to draw out the fibres as it falls and twist them together into long skeins

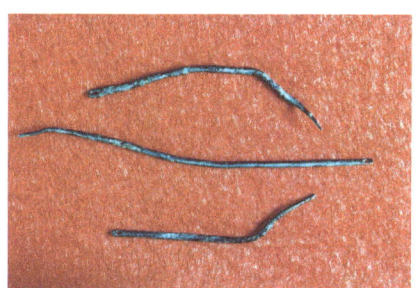

of yarn. The damage occurs when the whorl hits the ground too hard.

Broadly speaking, the ancient world was divided between high- and low-whorl societies. In Egypt and much of the Levant women used high-whorls; in Anatolia and Greece low-whorls were the go. Two deeply embedded domestic work practices, transmitted from mother or aunt to daughter or niece. But not often grandmother to granddaughter, for most women would have died before this was possible.

There was a similar divide in weaving, where horizontal looms were common in the high-whorl areas, while warp-weighted vertical looms were used elsewhere, including Cyprus. This crafting tradition of textile production was brought to the island, along with other crafts, by women coming to the island and developing the local Bronze Age cultural system.

We don't know much of the use of textiles, although a few scraps survive, or occasionally can be seen when embedded in corrosion on metal items once wrapped in cloth. We do have needles, quite long ones, and can pretend that some of the decoration on highly schematic female 'plank figurines' might represent woven patterns on their dress.

Spinning and weaving might have taken up some of women's time. But they had far harder tasks to perform. One of these was grinding wheat or barley into flour. This was heavy work indeed. The grain was ground on large

8. Observing crafty women

stone querns, crushed beneath the upper grindstones or rubbers, weighing, on average, nearly 6 kg. That's a heavy thing for a small Bronze Age woman to work with for hours at a time, forcing it back and forth across the quern. Gradually upper rubbers wore out, getting thinner and thinner, especially as every so often the grinding surface had to be refreshed, roughened up with a special stone pounder so it could do its job properly. At a late stage of its life the ends might hang down on either side of the quern, until eventually the rubber became too light or would break in two.

And so at least some of the ingredients for the family meal were ready. The flour could be baked in a small oven or made into a porridge. We found evidence of many other ingredients: legumes and fruit, meat from sheep, goat, cattle and the occasional hunted deer, milk (could they have made cheese, or an ancient Cypriot equivalent of modern *trachanas*, a dried milk and flour soup-stock). But what the recipes were is anyone's guess. Cooking pots (another Bronze Age innovation) were made of special clays and shaped to minimise thermal shock when heated and cooled. Some are small, perhaps for special foods or individual meals. Others are larger and could feed a family with soups, stews or gruel.

In our first season at Marki we were very puzzled by some very odd bits and pieces which we could not understand at all. They looked like distorted, decorated feet, and we'd never seen anything like them before. (Later we realised why: it was because most previous excavations had focussed on cemeteries: there was no call for these types of domestic utensils or installations in tombs.) Our first attempts to put our fragmentary ones together were laughable, but in later years we began to find many more complete examples, and we could see that they were pot-stands: hobs placed around the heath on which the cooking pots could be set over a small fire. Some were free-standing and portable, others were built-in. They were sometimes decorated

42

8. Observing crafty women

with incised patterns, like those on the spindle whorls or finer pottery, and sometimes they were reminiscent of the faces of 'plank figurines'. This resonance may not have been fortuitous, and we could, if we wished, make up a plausible story, seeing the hobs as symbolically associating women with the hearth, the home and centre of family life.

P14040 is a large storage jar. During one of the earliest episodes of occupation at Marki it was set upright in a large pit dug through the shallow earlier cultural deposits and deep into the natural soil below. Unusual enough in itself, but what was inside was even more unexpected. Once we removed the light, loose clean fill we came across the fragile skeleton of a small child – an unwelcome, indeed distressing, surprise. Although human remains turn up occasionally in settlements of the period, almost everyone – men, women and children – was buried in underground tombs

in nearby cemeteries. Why a few individuals were left or even formally buried in among the houses is a question we cannot answer, much as we'd like to know. Were these strangers with no kin in the village? Were they cases of accident or disease or maybe even something more sinister? With our two-and-a-half year old the use of the storage jar was especially puzzling. You can invent as many scenarios as you like: perhaps there was a distant memory of jar-burials in ancestral societies; perhaps the grieving mother could not bear to have her little one removed from the house, although that may be unlikely as so many children would have died in infancy or early childhood.

Our toddler had one particular feature that particularly excited Kirsi Lorentz, our bone specialist. The fragile skull had, in her technical words, 'clear anterior-posterior reduction in cranial dimensions'. In other words, the back of its very plastic skull had been flattened by being pressed against a hard back-board. This form of head-shaping, as in other contemporary examples Kirsi had studied, was due to the use of a particular form of cradle-board. We can see this in some models and figurines of women holding their tightly swaddled babies. The result was a regular, although not universal, feature found on many people of the time. It may even, as in some societies, have been intended to enhance their looks or to serve as a marker of status or identity.

This little, nameless toddler also reminds us — as if anyone needs reminding! — that our busy Bronze Age women were also mothers, carefully strapping their precious babes onto their cradle-boards to be carried around, laid down on the ground or propped up nearby while they, together with their sisters and cousins, went about their many other tasks within the village or out in the fields. Not their mothers, however, as they would probably not have lived long enough to enjoy many grandchildren.

9
Time and change

'*How old is it?*'
Often that's the first question archaeologists ask. They worry all the time, and especially about time — or at least I do. We often say the great advantage that we have over conventional history is that we deal with very long periods and the far distant past. But, if the truth be known, we really don't know how to understand such vast, incomprehensible stretches of time, way longer than individual lives, encompassing innumerable generations. We are, here as in other things, also very dependent on practice and evidence, and all too often by our own preconceptions.

From the middle of last century knowledge of the past has been revolutionised by radiocarbon dating. The age of bits of charcoal could now be measured, things could be independently dated: with more research, more excavations and more dates the past could be seen in new and better perspective. We see this dramatically when addressing so seemingly simple a question as 'When did people first arrive in Australia?'. Of course for some First Nations people the question may be irrelevant; for others putting a science-based number to their Ancestors' history is both socially affirming and of political value. But for me, it is important in the global history of our species and to investigate Aboriginal Ancestors' long, local history set against environmental changes over many millennia. But the actual number — how many years ago — is by no means fixed. Once excavated heritage places could be dated, this long history could be demonstrated. In the 1950s only (if 'only' is really an appropriate term!) a few thousand years; then, from the 1960s more than 10,000 years, back into the realms of the last Ice Age. By the 1970s there were dates of 20,000, 30,000 and then 40,000 years ago. Now, many accept a date as old as 65,000 years, although personally I am not quite so convinced by the available information and would be happier to say '50,000 to 55,000 years. What is important is that, if we

9. Time and change

play by the archaeological rules, we have to change our ideas as new evidence becomes available, but at the same time cannot go beyond the evidence however tempting it may be to do so.

But where do dates come from? A more personal example. In the 1970s the then Victoria Archaeological Survey excavated several rockshelters in Gariwerd (the Grampians) in western Victoria. At that time fairly large quantities of charcoal were needed for radiocarbon dating. The best that could be used didn't come from the very lowest part of the shallow deposits. But they had to do. These showed use of the shelters at about 3,000 years ago, give or take a few hundred years. Others used this information as a key argument for significant social changes across western Victoria at about that time. And that was what the the evidence – the dates which we all, perhaps too uncritically, accepted – did seem to show.

In the 1990s Caroline Bird and I, in a collaborative project with Aboriginal Affairs Victoria and local Traditional Custodians, undertook to re-examine the material from the excavations. By that time new techniques of radiocarbon dating had been developed: we could now date very small bits of charcoal, including those from soil samples stored since the excavations twenty years

9. Time and change

before. We didn't expect anything other than a confirmation of the previous dating. But we were in for a surprise.

One shelter, Drual, was shown to have been used over 20,000 years ago and another, Billimina, at least 15,000 years ago, and probably for some thousand years before that. A whole new history of the area was opened up, one where Aboriginal Ancestors were using Gariwerd during the height of the last Ice Age, when southeastern Australia was far colder and drier than today, and these ranges stood out from the surrounding semi-arid plains much as the Flinders Ranges in South Australia do today. New evidence: new histories.

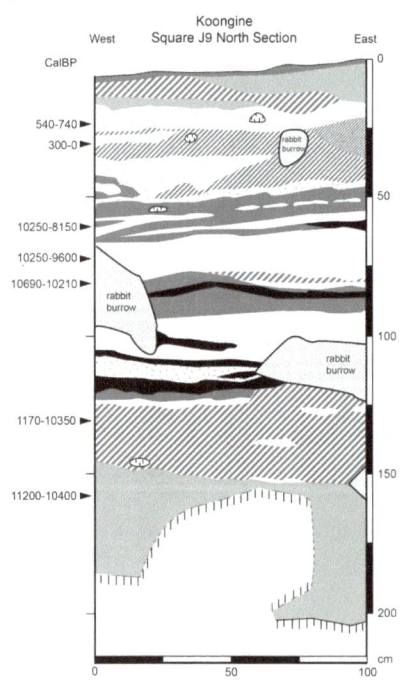

Another example, a bullet dodged! We dug a 2m deep hole through colourful stratified layers in Koongine Cave in South Australia and dutifully sent off samples for dating. Like all Australian archaeologists we could guess, sometimes more successfully than others, what the results would be. One charcoal sample came from the bottom: about 12,000 years ago. Good. Another from near the top: less than 1,000 years. Also good. And a third, about half-way up: 4,000 years. No problem. Taken at

47

9. Time and change

face value — and if these were the only three dates we had — it would have looked like the cave was used regularly with deposits accumulating slowly from 12,000 years ago until very recently, for no-one would have questioned so straightforward a sequence of dates. That would have been the site's accepted history, misleading us and future researchers. But . . . fortunately, these were not the only samples sent off. Another from the same location as the 4,000 year-old sample provided a date of about 10,000 years old! And, not far below the surface, another sample gave a similar, only slightly younger date. Just to be sure we sent off extra samples. These confirmed that the 4,000 date was anomalous, for whatever reason it was simply wrong — this happens, not infrequently. We now could be sure that the cave was only (!) used for about 1,000 years, certainly less than 2,000 years, Of course that is still a very, very long time indeed — perhaps as many as 80 generations. Almost by accident (but we can take some credit this time) we didn't provide entirely misleading evidence. Instead we have a different, we believe correct, history, and could then develop stories to explain why the cave started and then stopped being used sometime toward the end of the last Ice Age. It has to do, we suggest, with rising sea levels and associated changes to the distribution of resources in the surrounding area. Evidence is what you have, and is not always perfect.

This can be seen in a third example. It has to do with coastal shell middens, but has broader implications.

If you count up the relative number of radiocarbon dates from excavated middens there is a clear trend toward more dates over the last few thousand years. This can, and indeed has, been read as demonstrating an increase in the number of middens and therefore an ever-greater use of coastal resources in the recent past. A significant observation. *But is it right?* I don't think so. Let me explain why.

Coastal shell middens are particularly vulnerable to the impacts of wind and weather (see also Story 27). Mobile dunes shift and shell deposits can easily be degraded, if not destroyed. The older they are the less likely they are to survive — and if they do survive they are often in very poor condition indeed: perhaps merely a few scattered broken fragments. Now we

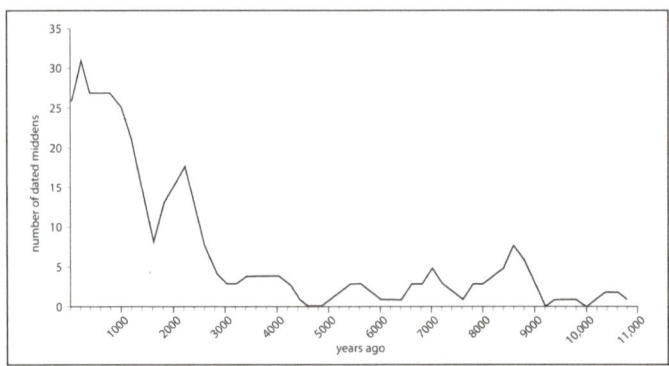

need to add in another factor: who obtained the dates, and why? Given the opportunity to excavate a midden, I'm sure that you, like any normal archaeologist, would choose a better-preserved one over a very poor example – especially if your interests were in understanding ancient collection strategies and economic behaviour. So, now it seems obvious, most dates come from middens excavated with a particular set of questions in mind, and so unintentionally avoiding those most likely to be old in favour of younger examples. To natural factors affecting survival we can add research bias. So, perhaps the upward trend in numbers does not reflect historical developments in the past at all. A bit of a worry, that.

Of course we can test this alternative explanation by dating shells from otherwise neglected, scrappier-looking scatters. So I collected shell samples from a range of poorly preserved middens on the coast of western Victoria and South-East South Australia. While dating experts and laboratories aim for high precision, if you only want to know the age to within a few thousand years, you can be less fussy – and save on the high cost of conventional

dating. Andrew Story and I, with help from colleagues in the Chemistry Department, tried out a cheap and nasty home-brand method, adequate for our purposes.

While some of my samples were relatively recent, half were over 4,000 years old,

49

9. Time and change

with one older than 8,000 years. Enough, I think, to show that the apparent pattern of an increase through time is certainly questionable if not entirely misleading. Another reminder that we always need to critically evaluate where our data come from!

Since then others, using proper dating techniques, have confirmed that people were collecting shellfish in the area from the time, about 10,000 years ago, when the rising seas approached the modern coastline. And presumably well before that.

Now a fourth example, a little different again, but staying with shell middens. Here we chose to excavate the well-preserved deep stratified layers in a midden at Moonlight Head on the rugged Otway coast in western Victoria. No problems with the dates this time, but let's think about what we do with them, and how we think about history. Initially, in order to link all the different areas excavated we divided the site into four periods of use, each about 200 years long. 200 years is a relatively short time in this type of archaeology, and doesn't compare with 20,000 or even 2,000 year-long sequences. It is perhaps only a matter of eight or ten generations. This was not an unusual thing to do, quite within normal archaeological practice. We'd sorted, counted and weighed all the thousands of shells, and played different games with them. One useful measure was to assess the diversity of species in each of the four periods we'd defined: did people change their collecting and eating habits through time – a history, if you like, of economic decision-making, where Aboriginal Ancestors decided whether a broad range of species was a better option than targeting particular types, choosing between easy-to-collect smaller ones or larger sized shellfish which were harder and more expensive to find. A pattern emerged. Patterns always will.

We can summarise these different approaches to collecting collection strategies. To understand this you'll need to look at three diagrams plotting time from left to right and the relative diversity from bottom to top.

The first diagram (a) shows each of the four main chronological units: this is how we initially presented, analysed and discussed

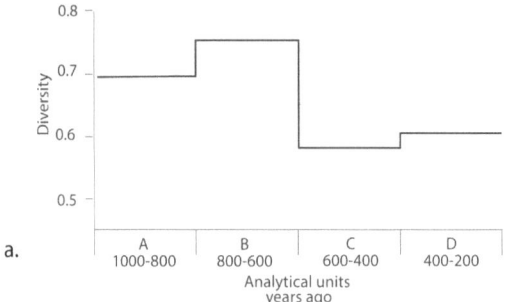

the sequence at the site.

But some years later I had doubts about how useful this was. How could I — or you, or anyone else — explain the sudden, instantaneous shift from one 200-year long strategy to the next?

So I tried something different. Keeping just to one part of the site I could use all the finest layers we'd separrated during excavation. Instead of four 200-year-long blocks of time, I could divide the sequence into 27 different units, as seen in diagram b. There are still changes, and they seem, especially when, as here, the connections between specific measures are smoothed out, and so give an impression of cumulative, directional change, first in one way and then in another. It looks like an understandable

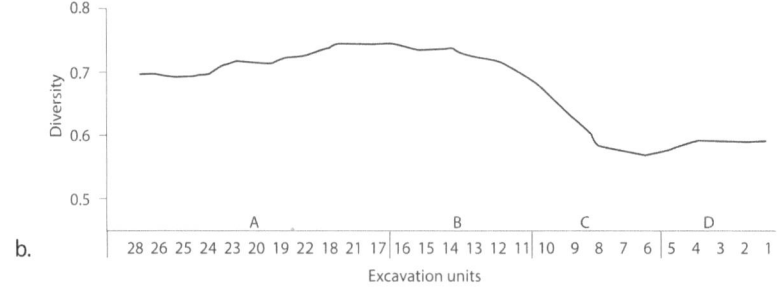

9. Time and change

process of gradual shifts in collecting or consumption strategies. Much better, I thought.

But now I am equally unhappy with that story. What if we don't join the dots? Then we have our 27 events isolated from each other and spread over some 800 years, as seen in the third graph (c). That is, showing about one event every 30 years — let's say once every generation. Of course the place must have been used more often than that as only a part of the midden survives and even less was excavated. But still. What we now see is not a history of development, but a series of independent activities, each unrelated to the one before or the one after. It is a different view, not concerned to explain change as is common in much archaeological discourse. Rather it shows unpredictable, perhaps opportunistic use of coastal resources at that particular place. It is a picture of the same general behaviour over many centuries, with small variations from one visit to another. Difference rather

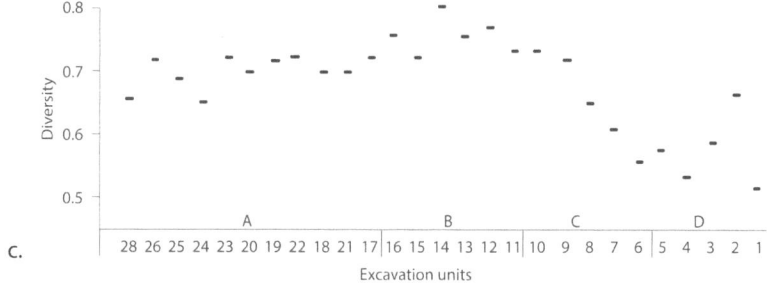

than change.

History comes in different ways and from different perspectives. Sometimes our archaeological dates behave themselves and neatly fit in with other types of evidence, providing different insights and mutual support. One example comes from close to home. Melbourne sits on the northern shores of the very extensive but relatively shallow Port Phillip Bay — Naarm to Bunurong and other Traditional Custodians. The Mornington Peninsula, which forms the eastern shore of the bay, is part of Bunurong Country, while the western side is Wadawurrung Country. As well as their own ongoing traditional knowledge, Aboriginal traditions of the area were occasionally collected by Europeans in the 19th century. One of these was mentioned by William Hull in what was hardly

9. Time and change

more than a casual aside in his testimony to a Select Committee of the Legislative Council in 1858:

> *The blacks say that their progenitors recollected when Hobson's Bay was a kangaroo ground. They say – 'plenty catch kangaroo and plenty catch possum there;' and that 'the river (Yarra) once went out at the Heads, but that the sea broke in, and that Hobson's Bay, which was once a hunting ground, became what it is.'*

Of course such stories were largely ignored for 150 years. Then geo-scientists looked closely at the contours and sediments of the bay floor (all to do with widening and deepening channels to cope with larger ships). They argued that sand-bars near the entrance had blocked off the sea about 2800 years ago, so that the bay dried out, becoming a wide, open plain, probably with a very salty lake in the central, lowest section. Then, a thousand years ago the sea broke through, the bay again filled with water.

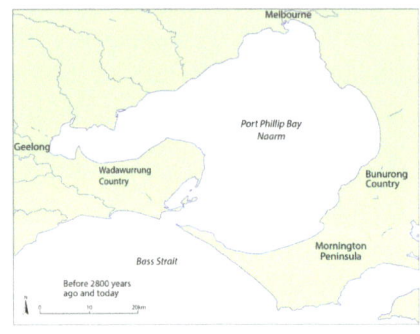

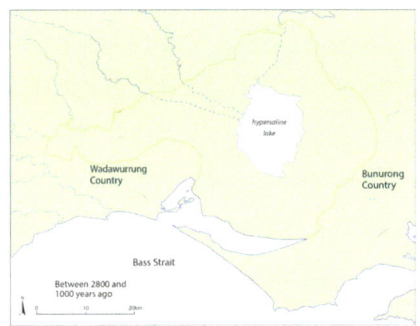

So, where do the archaeological dates and data come in? Obviously, when there was no water – and therefore no shellfish to gather – there should be no shell middens. Many of these Aboriginal places have been documented along the shores of the Mornington Peninsula on Bunurong Country. There are 73 radiocarbon dates from 27 of them. It isn't as easy as one might think to use the dates, especially those on samples of shell rather than charcoal, for old carbon hangs around for a very long time in sea water. As this is taken up by shellfish it affects the proportion of radioactive carbon isotopes, so dates need careful correction. This varies from place to place in complex ways. But with these

9. Time and change

technicalities dealt with the pattern of dates was just as expected, or at least hoped for. While the southern sections of the bay which did not dry up show a continuous presence of shellfish gathering, to the north middens only appear during the last thousand years. Perfect!

Once the barrier was broken through the valley would have rapidly begun to fill:

> *'Plenty long ago...men could cross, dry-foot, from our side of the bay [in the east] to Geelong [in the west].' They [the Aboriginal informants] described a hurricane – trees bending to and fro – then the earth sank, and the sea rushed in through the Heads, till the void places became broad and deep, as they are today.*

Although perhaps it was not as dramatic as suggested in oral accounts such as this, it would still have been rapid enough for Bunurong and Wadawurrung Ancestors to witness the drowning of these hunting grounds and for the event to be remembered for a thousand years.

We still need to work through all the many social and economic implications of this local environmental history, not only for the bay but for the area of what is now Melbourne and even beyond. When the bay dried out the loss of shellfish is most obvious. But, and perhaps more significant, would have been the loss of migratory eels, especially for those people, including Wurundjeri Woi-wurrung Ancestors whose country lies immediately to the north. For migrating eels and elvers could not swim across Naarm on their long journeys to and from breeding grounds in the Coral Sea far to the north. A serious economic and cultural loss indeed.

So, here our archaeological dates coincide with traditional knowledge and modern science to contribute jointly to a story of local environmental change and the continual adjustments required of Aboriginal Ancestors, for nothing in the world stays the same forever.

10
From one stone tool

Koongine Cave, December 1985. I am taking a video of Ken Mulvaney as he crouches at the bottom of a 1x1 metre square excavation just inside the entrance. He extracts one large piece of flint, hamming it up a little for the camera, and begins to gently flick off the attached soil. As he turns it over in his hands his self-conscious commentary gives way to a surprised '... it ... it's *beautiful*!'.

This stone tool – we'll call it '26/9'' – although, of course, it never had a name before – is now housed in the storerooms of the South Australian Museum. It is indeed quite a beautiful thing, a carefully shaped piece of fine-grained dark flint.

Open up your hand and spread out your fingers, trace an imaginary line around the outside of your palm and fingers. That's more or less its shape, straight across the end (where your wrist is) and with a continuous, very neatly chipped curve around almost all the rest of the perimeter. It's about half the size and thickness of my large hands, but not much bigger than those of my granddaughters. One side is smooth, the other is rougher with marks from its manufacture clearly visible.

We found 26/97 during excavations in Koongine Cave, near

10. From one stone tool

the coast south of Mount Gambier (we'll come to that later) for its life history began long before we enter the story — starting as an idea in the mind of Aboriginal man. *Yes,* it *could* have been a woman, although that is far less likely.

First – the raw material that it is made of.

Flint, some might call it chert, is a fine-grained, hard rock that forms as nodules or veins within limestone. It is ideal for making chipped stone tools, and was used, where available, by everyone's ancestors all around the world. Many of the beaches of the Lower South-East of South Australia are covered by masses of flint cobbles washed in from outcrops far out to sea. It is abundant and easy to collect. But it is not very good quality, and often has many impurities.

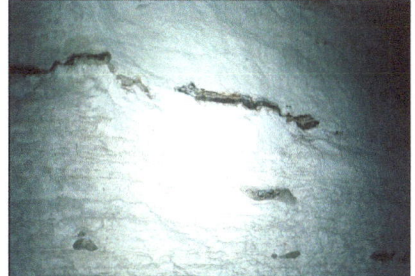

Far better quality flint can be found in the walls of the limestone sinkholes and caves so characteristic of the area. And, of course, as with many things, quality comes at a price — here involving more planning, organisation and effort and sometimes hours of difficult, perhaps backbreaking effort.

Several caves show signs of ancient quarrying. Some of these traces are deep underground, in dark cramped spaces. Tool marks show where masses of overburden were removed to expose the seams of flint. Here long, sturdy pointed stakes were used to split and remove the overlying rock. Then, working perhaps by flickering firelight, small groups of men gouged out hollows they could use to

10. From one stone tool

insert wedges to lever away the flint. Sometimes miners resorted to more aggressive battering, chipping pieces from all the nodules within reach up to several metres above the cave floor.

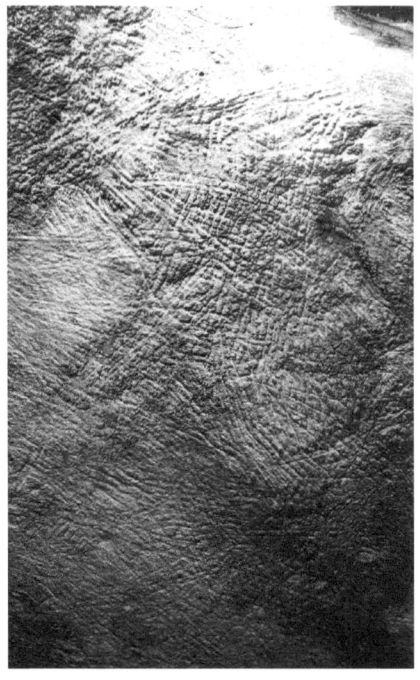

These caves also have markings on the walls: parallel series of finger marks or fluting impressed into softer limestone surfaces. The two activities — wall-marking and flint mining — may have been closely related. These markings are reminiscent of those found deep underground in almost inaccessible sections of Koonalda Cave, far below the surface of the Nullarbor Plain, where stone was quarried over 20,000 years ago. The Koonalda markings are very far removed in time and space from those near Mount Gambier. But perhaps they both belong to a very ancient, widespread tradition, somehow symbolically, even psychologically, linked to the underground mining

Once extracted the pieces of quarried stone could then be turned into tools. The stone for 26/97– our tool – may have been quarried in one of these other caves, but may, more conveniently, have been knocked off an outcrop in the wall of Koongine cave itself.

Wherever it came from, we can then see how the stoneworker went about his task — not by casual bashing, but through a thoughtful, careful process by an expert stone-knapper.

He (again, probably a 'he') would have turned the quarried piece of stone this way and that, sizing up its potential and deciding how best to prepare it so that a large flake of particular shape and size could be struck off.

10. From one stone tool

After some initial shaping he used his hard hammerstone to deliver a sharp blow in exactly the right place, at the right angle and with the right amount of force. Off flew the large flake that was to become 26/97. Satisfied with this product, our craftsman turned the flake over so that the smooth, inner surface of the flake was uppermost. Then, excess stone was removed by a series of lighter hammer blows around the perimeter. Detaching small chips from the underside created the curved convex edge, and gave the tool its final shape, with its robust but still sharp working edge.

A newly struck flake can be as razor-sharp as a sliver of glass — it'll slice your finger open, so never test its sharpness in that way! But such an edge will quickly become blunt, or snap and break away if used on harder material. Preparing a tool's edge for use requires a balance between sharpness and longevity, taking account of what it is to be used for.

Often the function of stone tools — or any other tools for that matter — can be identified from patterns of wear and damage, or by microscopic traces left on the edge. Our tool was designed for cutting and shaving wood. Maybe we should think of it as a hand-held adze: archaeologists prefer to use the more generic term 'scraper', or in this case 'steep edged scraper'.

Neat, well-made and useful though it was, 26/97 had a fairly short use-life. Then ... it was lost, or perhaps just

10. From one stone tool

left behind when its owner moved away from Koongine Cave. Together with other bits of stone and animal bone it was slowly buried as layers of sediment built up century after century. There it stayed until 1985.

That's when we began digging a small square shaft into the floor of Koongine Cave. We had no idea of how deep the deposits would be, what they would be like, or how old they were. Gradually a series of layers of different colour and texture were revealed, down to a depth of nearly 2m. Each had its share of tools, together with smaller chips from making or sharpening them and the bones of animals.

26/97 emerged about 75cm below the modern surface, from what we identified as our Layer 26 – hence the name. As we've seen, it was immediately recognised as something special, although it was far from the only tool of its type.

Large steep-edged scrapers with long curved working edges have long been known from the Lower-South East of South Australia. Their size and quality meant that they were particularly attractive to stone tool collectors in the middle of last century. Hundreds, sackfuls, were picked up by collectors from their favourite spots – such as the sandy exposures in the nearby Kongorong Hills. Only a small proportion found their way into public collections. Even so there are over 300 in Museum Victoria alone.

These large, steep-edged scrapers were identified as part of what became known as the 'Gambieran Stone Tool Tradition', named, obviously, from nearby Mount Gambier and seen as part of a regional type or style of tool, distinctly different from those of other areas.

But how old were they? As an understanding of Australian archaeology developed they were thought – as with other larger tool traditions – to be older than a range of smaller types typical of the last few thousand years. But nothing more specific was possible, as surface finds cannot be dated, especially when picked up with no thought to their context.

One clue came from excavations at Wyrie Swamp, not that far from Koongine. Here Roger Luebbers found similar types of stone tools in deposits which formed between about 12,500 and

10. From one stone tool

8,500 years ago. Even more important were other things of this age from Roger's excavations – for he found nearly three dozen wooden items. You can see them on display if you visit the South Australian Museum.

There are straight sticks with rounded and pointed ends used to dig up tubers from the soft muds on the ancient swamp margin. Spears were for hunting or, maybe, also for fighting: the best preserved of them is 120cm long, with

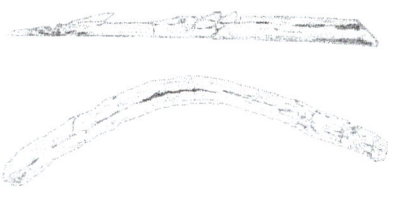

both ends sharpened. Two fragments have delicate barbs carved behind the tip. There are boomerangs, probably made of sheoak, which may have been returning boomerangs. They were made to be thrown across the swamp either to directly strike waterfowl or to frighten them into taking flight so they could be trapped in large nets, as was certainly done along the Murray in recent times.

The Wyrie Swamp wooden tools are by far the oldest we have in Australia, fortuitously preserved in the peat deposits. They not only show us what people were making and using at that far distant time but remind us of all the other organic items we will never find: things made of wood and bark, of skin, fur, sinews and feathers. The stone tools like 26/97 that we focus on are important today simply because they survive where most other things normally do not.

Back to Koongine Cave. Some time after we finished the excavations we received the results of radiocarbon dating of charcoal samples we had sent off for analysis. These fitted well with those from Wyrie Swamp, and show that most of the deposits in the cave built up over less than 2,000 years, from around about 11,000 years ago. Remember, of course, that even 2,000 years is a very long time indeed in human terms – perhaps 70 or 80 generations.

10. From one stone tool

We can imagine, then, that our tool 26/97 was used, like those at Wyrie Swamp, to cut, carve and shave wood to make a similar array of tools for similar purposes, especially to collect plants and hunt animals.

At Koongine we have no evidence of the plants that would have been harvested from the adjacent swampy wetlands. But there are many bones which come from a wide array of animals – kangaroo, wombat, wallaby, pademelon, possum, potoroo, bandicoot as well as reptiles and aquatic rats. They show that hunters worked across all the different nearby environments: open grassland, woodlands and wetlands. Small bits of emu eggshell tell us that people were certainly making use of the cave in the winter, if not at other times of the year as well. There were also a very few fragments of sea shell.

So we have one straightforward story – for some time, certainly less than 2,000 years or so, people often camped at or near Koongine Cave during the winter. Here they made stone tools and used them to carve other implements to help hunt and gather foods from their country. During one season about 10,000 years ago an Aboriginal Ancestor carefully shaped scraper 26/97, used it and then later accidentally left it behind or simply threw it away.

But there is more. Archaeologists are never really satisfied. They like to ask questions – perhaps more than anything else, except actually excavating! Those radiocarbon dates immediately raise two related questions.

One is why the cave was not used in earlier times – and the other – you can probably guess it – why did people no longer visit it by 9,000 years ago?

Our story then needs to move beyond the specific detail – to broaden out and take in the local, regional – and indeed global – context.

What of Koongine Cave itself? The name, by the way, was assigned to it by another archaeologist, making use of a word-list of the local Buandig language published in 1880 by Mrs James Smith. Her personal name was Christina, but as was normal practice of the time, she didn't use that in public.

Koongine Cave is set in a low limestone ridge running parallel

10. From one stone tool

to the coast, which is some 4km away. Before recent field drainage the land between the ridge and the beach dunes and flint pebble beaches was swampy, if not flooded. Today the cave is 10m wide and 25m deep, and the entrance too low to walk into with comfort, at least for someone of my height.

10,000 years ago, before the accumulating sediments filled it, the cave would have been wider, more open and with much greater headroom, making it a sizeable, perhaps even attractive place to shelter or to camp. We should also remember that while archaeologists like to dig in caves ancient people didn't necessarily prefer these natural shelters, for they can be dark, damp and uncomfortably constrained places.

But that is today. We need to go back to the very different worlds of the far distant past – well before Koongine was ever used.

18,000 years ago the last Ice Age was at its most intense. In the northern hemisphere glaciers spread across much of Europe. Here in Australia it was not quite so icy, but it was still cold, extremely dry and probably much windier than today.

Sea-levels were very much lower, because so much water was locked up in the expanded polar ice-caps. At that time you could walk from Victoria to Tasmania across a wide, flat plain, with a few low hills that we now see as the islands of Bass Strait.

Then, as the world warmed up, the ice caps melted. Sea levels rose. We should not in any way underplay the significance of the 1 or 2 metre rise in sea levels that modern global warming will bring with it. But this was a far, far greater rise – in the order of 120m

The Bass Strait was flooded, Tasmania cut off. And the map of Australia began to look more like that of today.

Where in earlier times Koongine Cave had been far inland, by 12,000 years ago the sea was coming closer. I like to think that at about that time extensive wetlands developed between Koongine's

10. From one stone tool

limestone ridge and the sea, with expanding woodlands further inland as vegetation responded to increasingly mild conditions.

The cave then became a convenient place to which people would regularly return, serving as an occasional base, for hunting and collecting in the surrounding area during the winter months.

The sea, then 10 to 20 km away, also provided useful resources, notably shellfish. If more recent times are any guide, camping in the dunes close to the beach was more of a summer-time activity, as anyone familiar with the Bass Strait coast will appreciate. From these places people could also make use of the extensive coastal wetlands that lay between the beach and Koongine's limestone ridge.

The sea continued to rise, coming ever-closer to its present location only a few kilometres from the cave. Beachside activities continued, but now the full extent of the wetlands could be accessed from camps in the dunes, while other resources could easily be reached from the higher ground inland. The ideal location for inland campsites was perhaps no longer beside the strip of wetlands, but further into the hinterland. Koongine Cave was no longer so convenient or attractive a place. So, people simply stopped using it.

Of course you may prefer a simpler, more pragmatic explanation. As the cave filled with sediments there was less and less headroom until it became too low to be comfortable to walk into it. You decide!

As time passed, tools like our 26/97 were no longer made and used. The Gambieran Stone Tool Tradition came an end. This does not mean that new peoples arrived in the area, but rather that new tool-types, made with slightly different techniques, were introduced and replaced the older fashion.

A Buandig legend reported by Christina Smith describes the way in which once extensive hunting grounds were flooded as the sea swept in to form the present coast. Could this story have at its core an extremely ancient oral tradition stretching back so many thousand years? The slow encroachment of the rising seas translated into a more catastrophic story? *Perhaps* .... perhaps I will one day fully overcome my inherent scepticism.

Some of the later Buandig ancestors, descendants of our

10. From one stone tool

toolmaker, were also among the very few — perhaps even the very last — people in Australia to see an active volcano when nearby Mount Schank erupted some 5,000 years ago. That, too, may underpin local creation stories which identified volcanic  cones as earth ovens used by the ancestral being, Craitbul.

If so, they may also demonstrate both the great longevity of an oral tradition over thousands of years and a continuity outlasting environmental changes and the consequent adjustments of local patterns of land use as well as innovations in language and in mundane fashions and techniques, such as those used to make our Gambieran scraper number 26/97.

11
Bull in a china shop

It is really my favourite museum. Comfortable and cool, the old Cyprus Museum in Nicosia houses many long familiar things, and a walk through the galleries is always a chance to visit old friends, especially the dozens of people from an ancient sanctuary at Ayia Irini. There they stand, big and small, pointy hats on their heads, many with one hand raised as if to say 'hello' and smiling their archaic smiles, as if in greeting.

Originally the four main sides of the museum surrounded an open courtyard. That must have been a shady place to escape the summer heat. But, in the middle of last century, the courtyard was roofed over to provide storage for the ever-increasing quantities of newly excavated material, stacked on trays slotted into place in rank after rank of tall, glass-fronted cabinets.

For many years, a privileged few scholars and students could pass through the heavy grey doors, and down the ramp laid over the worn stone steps into the dim long central corridor running between the dusty stacks. Toward the end of it there might be a small rickety wooden table or two where they could sit and study, by the dim light of an ancient reading lamp, whatever esoteric things they were researching. Here they were served by generations of ever-helpful museum staff, as friendly as those ancestors from Ayia Irini, and who, after long apprenticeships,

11. Bull in a china shop

could produce any item from whichever hidden corner it had been secreted.

A few years ago a new students' area was prepared, well away from the cluttered, busy, dark corridor: lighter, brighter and far more convenient. It was here that tray after tray of pots and sherds were brought up to us, as day after day we examined, described, drew and photographed the finds from

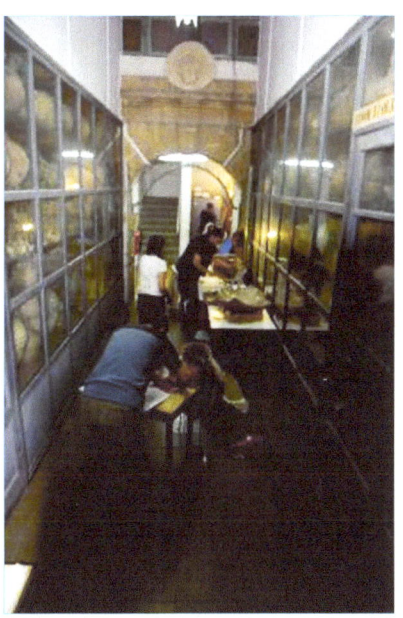

excavations at Ambelikou.

It was copper miners who found it. The Hellenic Company of Chemical Products and Manures, looking for new sources of copper ore, began to work on the top of a high hill near Ambelikou village. In their shafts and adits the miners came across discarded scraps left by ancient predecessors, some, unexpectedly, of the Bronze Age. Porphyrios Dikaios, then the acting Director of the Department of Antiquities was immediately excited. Recognising the importance of the finds he sent off his well-trained team to what was then a distant

11. Bull in a china shop

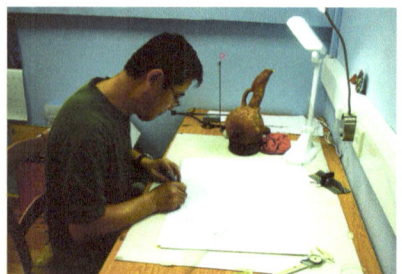

place, several hours difficult drive from Nicosia. He himself could only visit on occasion, for he could spare little time for fieldwork. Later, Ambelikou slipped well down the list of his many major projects and he was never able to complete his usual substantial study, although this was surely intended as dozens of smashed pots were carefully mended by museum staff.

Ambelikou was not entirely forgotten, but it remained a shadowy site on the fringes of archaeological consciousness, only the report of mining, a crucible and a casting moulds ever remembered as evidence of the earliest copper production on the island.

Eventually, our colleague Robert Merrillees thought to address this deficit. He focussed on the archival evidence and conscripted Anne-Elizabeth Dunn-Vaturi to process the finds. Their project stalled, until one day Robert suggested to Jenny Webb and me that perhaps we could take it over. 'Interesting, if not very exciting', we thought, 'a fairly straightforward salvage job. No worries'. Anne-Elizabeth and Robert generously gave us what they had done, and with the permission of the Department of Antiquities we set to work. While no written notes could be found there were the old negatives, some more useful than others, some section drawings of the layers of fill and large, carefully drawn plans. As we unrolled these a whole new vision of the site sprang out.

Two main areas had been excavated. One was clearly used for processing copper – it was where the old mould had come from,

11. Bull in a china shop

along with an array of heavy stone pounders for crushing ores and other related features and equipment. Unique, yes; important, yes; but, to me at least, not so interesting, despite my father being a Professor of Applied Geology and often concerned with mining.

The other area was the real surprise. The plans and photos revealed an unexpected view of a dramatic moment in time — a catastrophic event with dozens of pottery jugs lying scattered across the floor.

What was this?

Whether it was a careless accident, or perhaps an earthquake, a fire swept through this space one summer day nearly 4000 years ago. Storage shelves crashed down, taking their loads of tall jugs with them. We tossed around different explanations, but there was really no alternative to seeing this as a pottery-making workshop. All the jugs must have been the last kiln-load to be fired, stored ready for distribution. Other features and pottery vessels were those used by the potters, still in place.

Using the plans and photos, and not a little imagination, we can create a view of the workshop. In the foreground are large jugs and a stone basin, perhaps used to store

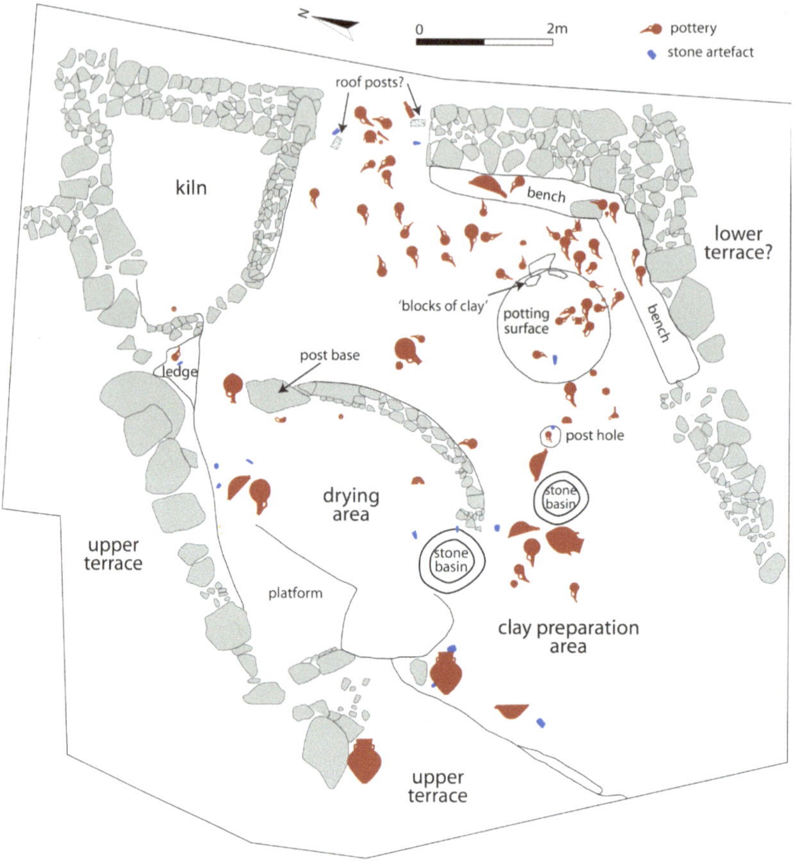
N
0
2m
pottery
stone artefact
roof posts?
kiln
bench
lower terrace?
'blocks of clay'
potting surface
bench
post base
ledge
post hole
drying area
stone basin
stone basin
upper terrace
platform
clay preparation area
upper terrace

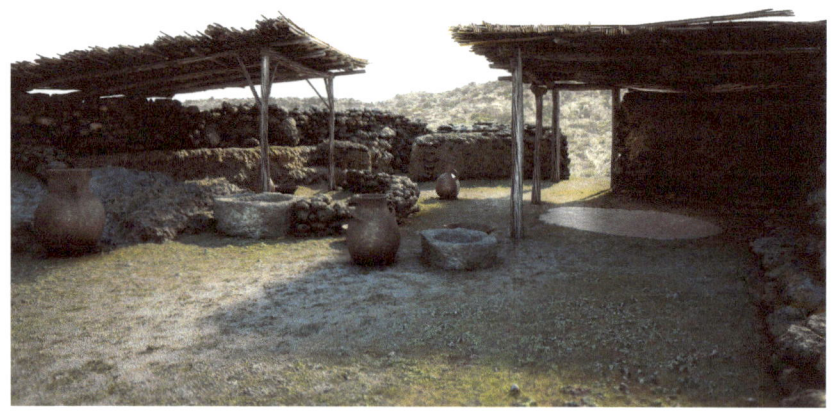

11. Bull in a china shop

clay and water necessary in working it. The circular platform to the right, shaded by the light roof, would have been where the potter sat: some slabs of clay, prepared already for making the next batch of pots, were found beside this area. To the left of the doorway was the square-shaped kiln. No doubt when in use the whole area would have been far messier and cluttered than in our neat reconstruction, full of activity, heat and noise.

Porphyrios Dikaios, one of the finest archaeologists Cyprus has produced, knew this already, but he only mentioned the potter's shop in passing in a general article on 'wartime discoveries' in the *Illustrated London News* in 1946, with a picture identifying the kiln. He never referred to it again, and to all our shame, for half a century no-one else noticed — although it was, quite possibly, in James Stewart's mind when he wrote that pottery production was 'too large to have been delegated to the women of the household and it is legitimate to visualise potters' shops' (I hesitate to suggest that he didn't mention Dikaios or his site by name because the two were at the time engaged in an awkward squabble over the origins of the Bronze Age –see Story 28). I, for one, had spent many years trying different ways of working out how Bronze Age pottery was made, and who made it. Did they use kilns, who they were? Should we think of individual women providing for their own households? Or, perhaps it was a few more skilled part-timers, making pottery for themselves and their neighbours? Or were there more complicated, more industrial arrangements of manufacture and distribution? The workshop at Ambelikou might not have all the answers, but certainly would have changed the nature of decades of debate.

That last firing had included 39 jugs of similar general type, some larger, some smaller but all with tall cut-away necks. Most were badly burnt and smashed to pieces where they had fallen, later painstakingly restored by Cyprus Museum staff soon after they were found. Although made at the one time, no two are exactly unlike. This was not just because they were hand-made (the potter's wheel was not used in Cyprus at this time) but each had a slightly different arrangement of little attached knobs or other decorative elements on the body or neck, with variations in the simple patterns incised on the back of some handles. People wanted standard items, but not boringly uniform ones.

11. Bull in a china shop

Its copper production connected Ambelikou to other parts of the island, and through them to the wider Mediterranean world. Perhaps its pottery, too, found its way to other villages, and certainly some pottery was brought to it from elsewhere – strands in a complex of economic and social relationships between communities.

Although we have been lucky enough to bring the excavations at Ambelikou out of the shadows, the site itself remains beyond our reach. Situated in the Turkish-controlled north of the island, it is now, as it has been since the invasion in 1974, simply not accessible. There is so much more we don't know about the Bronze Age activity on that hilltop, so many questions about the short-lived history of the settlement, about mining and metallurgy, the other industries and more ordinary, domestic life. It would be a site well worth further research, and, if I were younger and the political issues resolved, it would certainly be somewhere I'd be happy to spend my time, looking through this window into the lives of these potters, miners and farmers.

12
A mild obsession

It was really quite by chance. The book was in a sale at the university bookshop, mixed in with a random assortment of other remainders. The colourful illustrations felt vaguely familiar and I was intrigued enough to take it home, although I had no particular interest in biblical illustrations. These ones, I soon saw, were pictures embedded in my memory from many a Passover *Seder*. Some of the family *Haggadot* – the text read each year during this annual celebration of the Exodus before getting on to the chicken soup and gefilte fish – were illustrated with the same scenes as in this book of Christian imagery. This sparked an exploration in a field quite outside my prehistoric comfort zone, occasional, intermittent forays into a different world.

In particular, my *mishugas* – a mild obsession – focussed on the figures of the Four Sons. The *Haggadah,* ostensibly the story of the Exodus from Egypt, does not present a straightforward narrative.

12. A mild obsession

Instead it combines varied strands of different ages and types, all woven together into a pattern featuring teaching and learning, questioning and debating. The short section on the Four Sons (if you wish you could read this as 'children', but for 2,000 years it has always been just 'sons') is one of the oldest strands, predating Herod's rebuilding of the Temple in Jerusalem. Several biblical passages allude to passing on information from one generation to the next. Ancient rabbis extrapolated from these to discuss how one should explain the significance of Passover to children of different abilities: one wise, one wicked, one simple and one who does not even know how to ask. Think Marx brothers.

These four characters (or characteristics) have long been a favourite subject for illustration, often providing a visual, sometimes light-hearted, commentary or interpretation. The set I became obsessed with has the four side by side: Wise, old, bearded, learned; Wicked, a soldier; Simple, a dopy youth; and the last, a young child, and so combining behaviour and age-related explanations.

My question — and remember, the *Seder* and the *Haggadah* are all about questions — was 'where do these particular images come from?'.

The immediate answer was not hard to find. The originals of the familiar pictures were taken from an influential *Haggadah* published in Amsterdam in 1695 with a second edition in 1712. Its illustrations were instantly taken up copied and recopied innumerable times over the last three centuries, and still appear, if somewhat blurred and smudged, in some cheap, or give-away editions today. These were the images I grew up with; familiar to me as they were to so many others, fully accepted as standard Jewish imagery.

12. A mild obsession

But that's just the start of it. The Amsterdam *Haggadah* illustrations were themselves copied from older originals. Early last century Rachel Wischnitzer, the doyenne of Jewish art history, traced them back to the work of Matthius Merian the Elder. He was a prolific craftsman, who engraved pictures for many a book of history and geography – indeed his name is still synonymous with German  travel guides. Among his best known engravings were those ins in an edition of Martin Luther's bible, published in Stuttgart in 1630. This included pictures also used in smaller books of biblical scenes – a popular genre of the time. His *Icones Biblicae*, published in 1625 (it was a coloured version of this that was to blame for my obsession) was one source; another was a massive history of the world compiled by Gottfried in 1619.

This conversion of Merian's Christian and secular images into Jewish ones is well known. They were prepared by Abraham ben Jacob, appropriately also a convert, who abandoned his life and career as a Christian pastor in the Rhineland and moved to Amsterdam to become an engraver in that burgeoning centre of book publishing.

-•⊱(אָב)⊰•-   39

אַבְרָהָם בֶּן יַעֲקֹב ABRAHAM ben JACOB, hunc LXXXIX b. verbi divini Miniſtrum fuiſſe in litoribus Rheni, & ad Judæos tranſiiſſe, ac nunc vivere Amſtelodami, ibique Mappam Geographicam de Palæſtina, in qua urbes Hebraicis nominibus inſignitæ ſint, edidiſſe, ex libro quodam, manu ignota notato, ſe didiciſſe ſcripſit mihi Cl. *Theodorus Haſeus*. Idem varias tabulas æneas Amſtelodami expreſſit, quarum nonnullas illuſtrat Cl. *Hardtius* in Ænigmatibus Judæorum religioſiſſimis pag. 2. ſqq.

When commissioned to prepare illustrations for the new *Haggadah* he chose to base them on the well-known work of Merian, modifying some scenes, rebadging others and, in the 17th century equivalent of cutting and pasting, transferring individual figures from one scene to another. There was no copyright control in those days, and artists and illustrators felt free to copy anything from anyone.

12. A mild obsession

Some scenes were simply reused: the Egyptian princess finding Moses in the Nile; the three angels visiting Moses and Sarah; the drowning of Pharaoh's army in the Red Sea. Others were given a different meaning, so that Merian's 'Romulus killing Remus', suitably adjusted, became 'Moses killing the Egyptian' (or in some later *Haggadot*, Hebrew slaves oppressed by an Egyptian taskmaster). A banquet scene, originally Joseph entertaining his brothers, was used to illustrate one segment of the *Haggadah,* recounting a debate between five Talmudic scholars at Bnei Brak. Could it be that it was initially intended to retain this original meaning, but instead was given the alternative reading by the publishers — a reading reinforced when the picture was further modified for the 2nd edition in 1712?

Back to those Four Sons.

Abraham ben Jacob didn't use a particular Merian original as a base, for none would have been appropriate. Instead he lifted his four sons from four entirely different places. My obsession became 'why these particular individuals?' Matthaus Merian produced hundreds, indeed thousands of engravings, many crowded with dozens of figures of all shapes, sizes and conditions, many of them perfectly suitable models. So, why these particular four?

It is not really a question of major significance, but that is not the point. Research — finding a plausible explanation — can be its own reward.

It was the Wise Son, naturally, who gave me an answer. He was the hardest of the four to find, and I wasted many hours fruitlessly searching for him. Eventually I recognised him in a picture in Gottfried's *Historical Chronicle,* where Merian engraved a scene of the Greek historian Herodotus receiving a crown of honour from Anytus, when he read his *Histories* to the people of Athens. Between the two is the young Thucydides, the equally great historian of the Peloponnesian War. He is shown there because, according to the *Suda* (something like a Byzantine forerunner of Wikipedia) he

was so inspired by Herodotus' reading that he decided then and there to emulate him and to become an historian. Thucydides was not, of course, our Wise Son. Instead the figure of Anytus was Abraham ben Jacob's model. It is not too much of a stretch to appreciate that the choice of this particular older, bearded figure, above all the numerous others of the same general type, was because of his association with this story of inspiring the young — illustrating a learning experience befitting a wise son, following the example of his elders. Here a text from the Classical world reinforces the traditional Jewish reference.

So, too, with the 'son who does not know how to ask'. Abraham ben Jacob's little boy was once Merian's child Hannibal, now suitably wearing a *kippah* or *yarmulke* on his head. Livy, the Roman historian, tells us that Hannibal's father Hamilcar *'led the boy to the altar and made him solemnly swear, with his hand upon the sacred victim, that as soon as he was old enough he would become the enemy of the Roman people'*. A father teaching a son, even if the message was not quite kosher.

The Simple Son. He used to be Merian's Saul. Not the grumpy king, but the younger modest and humble man, who hid 'among the baggage' when selected to become king, and, according to one Talmudic discussion, as free from sin as a one year old child. Beyond this childhood innocence, the choice of Saul may also reflect the major theme of searching and questioning as Saul here followed his father's instructions to seek out their lost animals. Once again there is an underlying allusion—a questioning and obedient young man— entirely in keeping with the context of the *Haggadah*.

12. A mild obsession

What of the Wicked Son? Often said to be a Roman soldier, he is in reality an Assyrian, copied from Merian's engraving of Sennacherib's plague-ridden army fleeing from Jerusalem. He is running from the wrath of God and from Jerusalem — rejected just as the Wicked  Son should be. He is a fairly stock figure, and appears again in Merian's illustration of the death of Absalom — that would be a wicked son indeed!.

And so, eventually, an itch scratched, a plausible link found. We see Abraham ben Jacob as a man familiar with Classical learning and history as well as both Christian and Jewish religious knowledge. Familiar too, with books illustrating both. Skilled at his craft, but perhaps without the confidence or imagination to invent new characters and scenes. Working for, and with, the entrepreneurial publishers of the 1695 *Haggadah* he was able to choose and modify images which were destined to last longer, perhaps, than their originals. And, may I suggest, with a quirky individual attitude that led to his choosing these four images with their subtle, varied associations for reasons that may never have been appreciated by anyone else.

13
You pays your money

Some things, just like some people, attract attention. One such thing is the 'Vounous model'. You've probably not heard of it before, but generations of those interested in the Bronze Age of Cyprus have had an almost irresistible compulsion to say something about it — including me. My very first publication on Cypriot archaeology half a century ago drew a connection between it, two models from Kotchati (in reality, probably Marki) and the carvings on the walls of Tomb 6 at Karmi (see Story 4) — and in doing so suggested that the Vounous model showed a funeral scene, representing activities within a cemetery. A mild enough suggestion, compared with many.

So, what is this model? It is made of clay; a roughly circular area, about 37cm in diameter, is surrounded by a low wall with an arched opening. A large seated man is clearly a focus of attention,

13. You pays your money

with other people, both men and women (one with an infant), around and about. There are cattle penned in small enclosures, and against the wall in front of the seated man is a relief feature: three uprights with a cross-piece from which hang wavy things. Beside the entrance someone is looking in at the scene. Plenty to keep everyone amused.

Porphyrios Dikaios found it in a Bronze Age tomb at Bellapais Vounous. In 1931 reports of looting took him to the site, where, along with the usual array of bowls, jugs and the like he found numerous fragments scattered on the floor of one chamber tomb, explaining that ...'*It seems that the looters who visited this tomb ... found this object not to their taste ... and broke it into many pieces*'. Fortunately enough survived, although the model needed extensive reconstruction before its form and detail could be appreciated.

Porphyrios immediately saw it as a significant find, and — as it did not conform to the rectangular form of contemporary

13. You pays your money

buildings, and on the analogy of later structures – decided it was an open enclosure, and not only that, but a sacred enclosure. Others were not slow to put in their tuppenny-worth. Within a year, René identified the vertical wavy relief lines as snakes, suggestive of a chthonic cult, of death and the underworld. At an international conference later in 1932 Porphyrios described his find as an 'elaborately modelled scene of worship, and symbols of mother goddess, bull, and snake'. Sir Arthur and (not-yet-Sir) John, both very senior English archaeologists of the time, disagreed and thought the scene was domestic rather than of a public ceremony.

And so it began. Porphyrios didn't change his opinion, maintaining the model '... *is an important representation of a ritual in honour of the dead (the model was found in a tomb) but also in honour of the associated god of fertility, whose attribute is the bull*'. Jim accepted the idea of a circular open-air shrine where animals were offered to the gods, suggesting a graded hierarchy in the ceremonies, with some people, like the one peeping over the wall, excluded from participation. Vassos, too, followed the explanation of the model as a sacred enclosure, but ignored the further interpretation of the cult; Desmond had a more prosaic view, seeing it as a simple village scene after a hard day at work; Marcia liked the idea of a funeral ceremony . . . .

And so it goes on, reflecting changes in the real world and archaeologists' preceptions and agendas. So, Eddie took a new line, arguing that the whole scene should be regarded as representing and legitimising the authority of newly emerging elites who were busy transforming and stratifying society into a more hierarchical structure; Sturt expanded on this, suggesting that the main figure is an individual 'aggrandiser' associated with symbols of status and power; Diane added a gendered perspective, with a marginalised woman with her baby keeping to her place in a ordered world of males, females and animals; Louise pointed to the varied sizes of the figures as a form of 'social perspective' portraying their different individual status, emphasising wealth and prosperity through cattle; Andrew focussed on the 'throne' on which the largest figure is seated, finding a parallel in some odd shaped blocks found in the same area as a burial at Alambra,

13. You pays your money

suggesting they fitted with the concept of mortuary ritual and also showed a level of detailed realism on the model.

Now we can add in Netice who told another story, seeing the model as a representation of a life cycle, starting with birth, marriage, having children and getting older. One group of figures then become participants in a marriage ceremony while the little figure peering over the wall is a frustrated, rejected suitor. Giorgos, however, saw him/her/it as a socially excluded 'peeping tom'. If we let our imagination run wild we could take this even further, developing yet another concept, with this alienated figure as the artist/potter and so — dare I suggest? — the earliest self-portrait in prehistoric Cyprus. *What do you think?*

Not that any of this will end at all soon. A few years ago Giorgos (another Giorgos) found fragments of what must be a similar model in a tomb in Nicosia — something, should it be needed, to stimulate even more speculation for another hundred years.

Meanwhile, *you pays your money and you takes your choice*!

14
Lime, chemistry and style

The Director of the Department of Antiquities had misgivings. The Australian High Commissioner stepped in with some extreme diplomacy and eventually we reached a workable solution. Giorgos Georgiou had asked us to help with a salvage excavation on the south coast. We were happy to oblige, but the joint operation needed clear lines of demarcation. The compromise: the Department would do the actual excavation, and we'd process the finds. Disappointing — who doesn't like digging? —but that's how it was. As it turned out, *what a relief!*

Giorgos and his team battled for weeks in the heat and dust to clear dozens of small, collapsed tomb-chambers cut into the soft limestone near Psematismenos Village. The chambers were filled with reconsolidated limestone which, over 4,000 years, had set like cement. The vessels within them were also filled and encrusted with a thick plaster coating, exhausting to find and difficult to extract. Each day they would return to the Larnaka Museum, caked with a thick dusting of fine lime powder. It was comparatively easy for us in the museum courtyard and storerooms, even though we struggled with acid-baths and improvised tools to remove the plaster from inside and outside the pots. Of course it was worthwhile, for between us we rescued an Early Bronze

14. Lime, chemistry and style

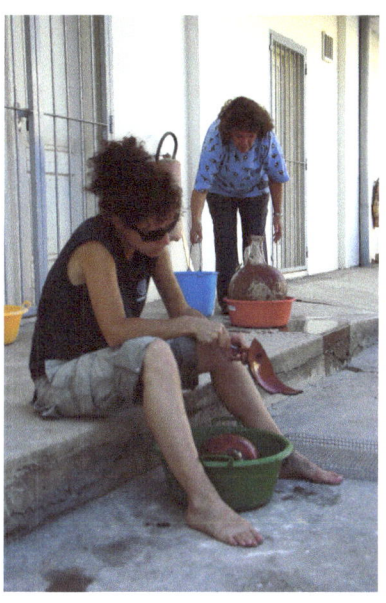

Age cemetery from the developer's bulldozers.

We knew far too little about that period in that part of Cyprus, but now we had a great deal of complete pottery, rivalling the major collections from tombs at Bellapais Vounous on the north coast, 60 or 70 km away. These had been excavated in the 1930s by a Frenchman, a Cypriot and an Australian — no joke, especially as none of them got on very well. We've picked up after two of them before: James Stewart at Karmi and Porphyrios Dikaios at Ambelikou.

It was immediately clear that our Psematismenos

pottery was quite different from what they had found at Vounous, although we'd label it all, not very imaginatively, as 'Red Polished Ware', because it is reddish in colour and rubbed smooth before firing to give a slightly lustrous sheen. These differences are not simply those you might expect to develop between local potters living at some distance from one another, but reveal something very different about the people they were made for. We'll come back to that in a moment, after a short detour to explain how we know that the two areas were in contact with one another. This involves a bit of applied technology (some pretentiously like to say 'science') but don't be frightened off, at least not yet.

Clays contain tiny traces of many elements, varying in presence and proportions from one place to another. If we can measure and compare these we can tell if pottery was made in the same place or not; or if special clay mixtures were prepared for particular types of pottery and so on. Until fairly recently this always needed the help of someone wearing a white lab coat to work a big machine of one sort or another, something slow and expensive. Now we have portable devices, looking for all the world like a Star Trek phaser, which can do the job adequately if not perfectly. An important advantage, apart from speed (you can measure hundreds of samples quite quickly) is that it is non-destructive, so museum curators don't get upset. These portable X-ray fluorescence analysers have become extremely popular, and archaeologists now point them at anything that doesn't move — hopefully not at anything that does, because they use a powerful beam of X-rays to excite and measure trace elements.

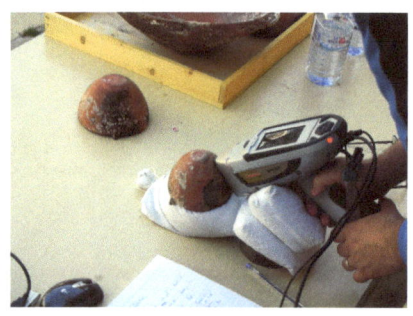

Well, we had one such new, shiny expensive toy in Cyprus, and zapped hundreds of our vessels from Psematismenos. We also did the same with the pottery from Ambelikou and later some from Vounous — pottery excavated by James Stewart which had made its way into the Australian Institute of Archaeology, which was,

14. Lime, chemistry and style

conveniently, housed at La Trobe University in Melbourne. All this meant was that we had a massive spreadsheet of numbers: how much rubidium, titanium, zirconium and whatnot was in each of hundreds of pots. Unfortunately to make sense of this we have play with numbers. One game which I like manipulates all that information and draws out and simplifies the main patterns within it, identifying those that explain most of the variation. The results can be presented on a graph. Have a look at this one — even if you don't like these things. You can see that the pottery from Vounous (red) and Psematismenos (green) is clearly separated: the clays in each area are different (don't worry about why, but there is a good reason). But, there is an interesting anomaly. In among the Psematismenos samples are two which come from Vounous. As it turns out, these, two bowls are different from the others from Vounous, much more like those from Psematismenos. They must have been taken from there, or somewhere nearby, to the north coast (and then 4,000 years later, brought to Melbourne). Some interchange of pottery — and probably other things, perhaps even people, took place.

So much for the analytical technology. The pottery itself is more interesting.

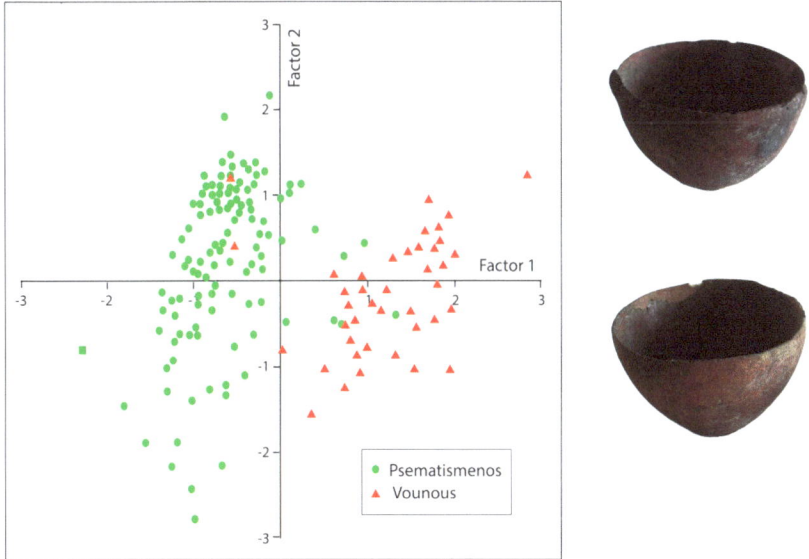

14. Lime, chemistry and style

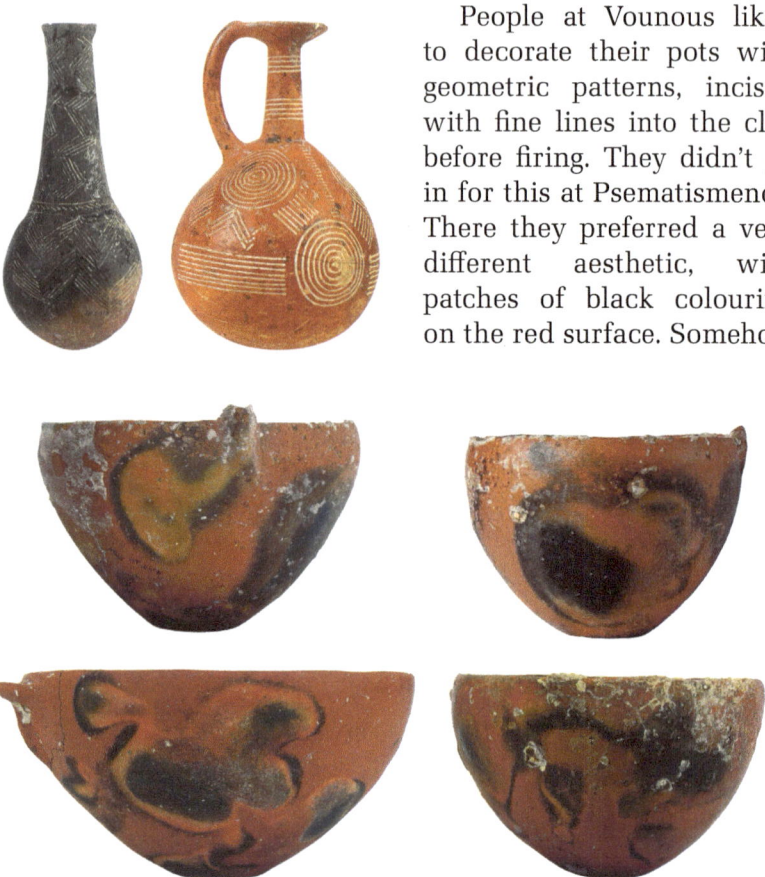

People at Vounous liked to decorate their pots with geometric patterns, incised with fine lines into the clay before firing. They didn't go in for this at Psematismenos. There they preferred a very different aesthetic, with patches of black colouring on the red surface. Somehow the potters achieved a deliberate mottling on the surface during firing, Although the exact form this took would always have been unpredictable it produced amazing complex, free-form and unconstrained patterns. What might this say about the overall approach to life in these two communities?

Or, a third example. The slightly later pottery from Deneia tells another story. Again within the same overall tradition, but assertively different. Like that at Vounous, the preference was for incised geometric patterns (of course it is difficult to do anything else with incision), but sometimes this was more deeply cut and bolder. The same approach can be seen with the heavy applied decoration on some of the larger vessels. Deneia saw a massive

14. Lime, chemistry and style

88

14. Lime, chemistry and style

expansion of population in the Middle Bronze Age, perhaps with people attracted to it from smaller villages, and it is tempting to see this local pottery style reflecting the need to identify with the new centre. Even so, there was always the counter pull toward individuality, for hardly any two vessels were exactly alike as you can see on the fragments of small bowls on the previous page. People of Early and Middle Bronze Age Cyprus always seemed to want something different.

Even so, this variability took place within a closely constrained tradition. The social rules governing decoration, like those for shape and surface colour, were very clear. Whether working within the in more formal local styles of Vounous and Deneia, or within the more relaxed, free-ranging mode at Psematismenos there were always limits to how far potters could diverge from well-established practices.

15
Not Elizabeth's boot-scraper

'Why dance jugs around a door-scraper?'
'But don't you see what it means, you — you dull-witted animal?'
cried the Rat impatiently.

In one of the finest examples of hypothetic-deductive reasoning in archaeology, the Water Rat then proceeded from initial observation to hypothesis, to testing, confirmation and further testing until his hypothesis was proved, and at last the Mole understood what that boot-scraper meant.

The boot-scraper we danced around was not ever lost from sight, but still had its story to tell.

We were at Elizabeth Farm House in Rosehill in 1972 – the start of an Adult Education course organised

by the late Ian Jack — I was responsible for the archaeological side of things and he for the associated historical research.

It didn't start off all that well. Very early on the first day I'd driven out toward Parramatta, nervously making sure my carefully prepared lecture notes and the magazine of 35mm slides were safely in the car. Arrival at Elizabeth Farm — the promised slide projector and screen were nowhere to be seen! — *panic!* — how to introduce archaeological procedures without pictures? But somehow, with a rickety, scrounged blackboard and scrap of

91

15. Not Elizabeth's boot-scraper

chalk, I made do. It became easier once we started to explore the house, and to work out what and where we could dig. There was little *why?*, for this was the early days of historical archaeology in Australia, and neither academic questions nor management and restoration considerations were at all well developed. But again, we made do. And, I like to think, didn't do too badly.

That boot scraper.

One of a pair set on squared stone blocks next to the front verandah seemed as good a place as any to begin; to explore an area of the front garden to see what we could see. At least it looked like a proper excavation, with neatly laid out squares extending across the grass lawn.

Not surprisingly, the front garden had seen many changes since the house was first built in 1793 for Elizabeth and John Macarthur, famous for merino sheep and the 'Rum Rebellion'. Different features were put in and removed over the generations, sometimes related to rebuilding of the house itself. The boot-scraper was obviously one of the latest additions, after a gravel circular carriage-way went out of use. And so on. Interesting enough.

Elsewhere our work was constrained by access. The building was being renovated at the time, so in some parts the floor-boards had been lifted, or could be removed. So our excavations

15. Not Elizabeth's boot-scraper

could in one place reveal older foundations, stumps for joists and bearers for earlier flooring; in another, post-holes and supports where there was once a light verandah; and under the front hall, a brick-lined, stone floored cellar, filled with rubble when it went out of use and the entrance was bricked-up, sometime after 1816 — a coin of King George III (he was the mad one) in the filling conveniently providing a date. The cellar must have been in use at least until then (did John store his rum in it?) but filled in some time after — how long after is anyone's guess: 10 years? 30 years?

The bits and pieces we found — coins, buttons, clay pipes and other small oddments — were stored, along with things from other excavations, in a space colonised by the newly formed Society for Historical Archaeology, in the 'Institute Building'. An exceptionally fine example of Victorian architecture, the New

15. Not Elizabeth's boot-scraper

South Wales Institution for the Deaf, Dumb and Blind (dreadful name! dreadful system!) has now been extensively restored and repurposed by the University of Sydney. But, after a long and varied career, in the early 1970s it was neglected and deserted, its dimly lit cavernous rooms a dumping ground for unwanted residues from everywhere and anywhere: an archaeological treasure-house, had anyone been interested. Here we discovered, to our surprise, a symposium of large Greeks. These full-sized plaster-casts of Classical sculptures had been ostracised – banished from the Nicholson Museum for the sin of being only copies. Not good enough for display, perhaps, but even in their sad and gloomy exile they provided me and my fellow students – deprived colonials that we were – with an unexpected opportunity to appreciate something of their size and three-dimensional form, so different from the small grainy black-and-white illustrations in the textbooks. Glimpses of the past, best experienced in the real world.

So too with the boot-scrapers at Elizabeth Farm. You can see them today standing at the entrance to the neatly polished House, a product of decades of ever more sophisticated concepts and techniques of restoration, management, public education and entertainment. One image out of a complex history of the building and its occupants.

16
Obsolescence

Archaeologists are very fashion-conscious, although you wouldn't think so if you ever saw one. They are quick to follow trends, adopting and adapting ideas and approaches, dressing their evidence to suit. In the late 1960s formal wear and numbers were all the go, for computers had come to town.

I'd spent a long time in the Cyprus Museum and elsewhere making notes on hundreds and hundreds of Bronze Age White Painted Ware bowls and jugs and such, from many sites. I now needed to do something clever with all this information. It seemed a good idea to try to calculate the similarity of the sites to one another in terms of their painted designs. This should, hopefully, be a measure of the social relationships between them. It was a fashionable thing to do, now that so many sums could be done by a computer. Sydney University had one. I was able to use it — just.

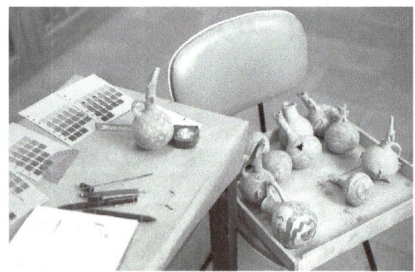

They tried to teach me FORTRAN, the language that the IBM 7040 spoke, but with little success, partly because the classes were run by mathematicians and I couldn't understand

16. Obsolescence

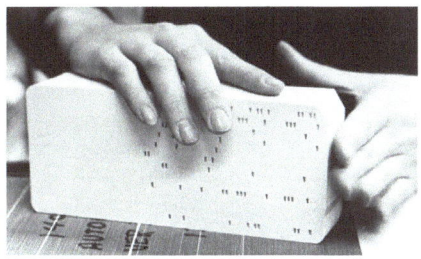

what they were asking us to translate. But, luckily, I found a book with programmes (we spelt it that way in those days) that I could use. All I had to do was tediously type out the fiddly instructions onto computer punch cards —a technology now more obsolete than many of those of the Bronze Age. And do the same for each of my many pots. No mistakes allowed!

It all took no little time — largely to correct tiny mistakes on the punch cards. I'd take my long box of hundreds of cards to the Basser Computing Centre at Sydney University and hand them over to an acolyte in a white coat: I never got to see The Computer itself. Then I'd walk to the university from our house in Camperdown the next day or the day after to see if they'd fed the machine with my offering and to pick up the answers.

Time after time the program failed, each time a bit further along when a comma or bracket or space was out of place or a DO-LOOP unresolved. But, one day, it all finally worked. Success!

One method I liked was 'cluster analysis' which archaeologists, magpies that we are, had picked up from biologists, who used it to classify birds, bugs and other creatures. It could also be used to classify artefacts on the basis of many attributes. It could also show the relationships between other things, like my Cypriot sites. Nowadays I — or indeed you — can do all of this almost

16. Obsolescence

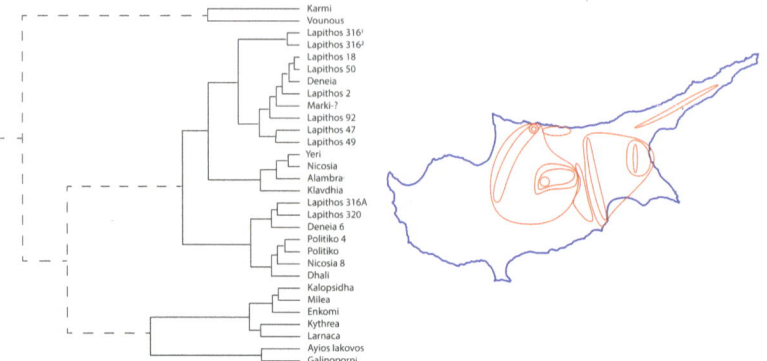

instantaneously on your laptop, and, for all I know, on your phone. But then the answers came out in text and not as neat diagrams, and so needed to be interpreted and drawn by hand. Then, finally, I could see the sort of patterns that I'd been hoping for. A bit of a shock, really, as suddenly it all seemed over: all that work and now what? All I needed to do was to write about it and to develop a good explanation for something seemingly obvious: the closest relationships were between those places which were nearest to one another. People talked more to their neighbours than to those further away. Big deal!

Those analyses. seemingly so important at the time (at least to me) are now themselves all but obsolete, overtaken by new evidence and a better understanding of the nature of the pottery industry and social relationships during the Middle Bronze Age. The overall approach, too, is hardly used, for fashions come and fashions go, and number-games have declined in popularity. New ways of thinking or new types of questions have developed – along with heartfelt sighs of relief by many, for archaeologists are often no more statistically minded than they are fashion-conscious and often can't go much beyond simple percentages.

97

17
A menagerie

'Who is the Potter, pray, and who the Pot?' asks Omar Khayyam's impatient vessel. One very small character in the British Museum certainly seems to have some confusion about its identity. Although this may be our lack of understanding rather than its personal problem.

There are quite a number of equally entertaining Cypriot Bronze Age people and animals in captivity in museums all around the world. One such menagerie is in Oxford, where they live in the Ashmolean Museum, hidden among all the more mundane items. It's not always quite clear what species they are, although one is certainly an ancestor of Dr Doolittle's Pushmi-Pullyu. You might be tempted to think of the one on the

17. A menagerie

upper left as a camel, but that is very unlikely so it is best, if not very helpful, to call it a 'zoomorphic vessel' or, even less usefully, classify it as WP IV Type XVIII.1. Some are recognisable, such as the little woman who was once attached to a large vessel, along with her sister and their donkey.

These oddities often receive more than their fair share of attention: I got to know these ones when working on the extensive collections in the Ashmolean Museum. Lena and I had never planned to be in England. But in July 1974 there we were, courtesy of the RAF, evacuated together with one-year-old Daniel as Turkish forces attacked the island. A personal disruption to our lives, but nothing compared to the on-going trauma afflicting all Cypriots, who, half a century later, still live with the consequences of the invasion on their small, divided island.

What to do with ourselves? Paul Åström suggested that I should prepare a publication on the major collections in the Ashmolean Museum and organised a continuation of what was left of my small Swedish stipend. The Curators kindly gave me the run of the Cypriot collections in their care, so I could busy myself with them as much as I wanted. A useful exercise, even if only as a form of occupational therapy, and a comfortable interlude for the rest of 1974, although with no certain future.

Eventually, nine years later, after moves to London and then to Melbourne, I was finally able to complete ink copies of the hundreds of drawings, printing all the photos, typing the text and laying out Volume 7 of Paul's *Coprus of Cypriot Antiquities* — one contribution to his vision of a comprehensive publication of as many Cypriot antiquities as possible. Twenty-three more volumes

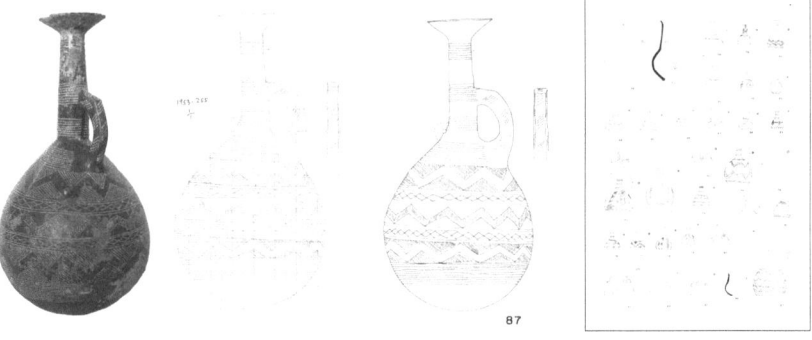

have been published since then, but this is still only a small fraction of the vast quantities of things which, thanks to a long history of looting, are to be found in almost every museum in the western world. The collections in Oxford are somewhat different from most as they include many things from excavations and professional surveys. These are far more useful to archaeologists than the masses of undistinguished pieces of unknown origin.

To publish all these was seen by some as pretty much a waste of time. An alternative approach places a different value on the material. Over many years the indefatigable Vassos Karageorghis encouraged many a museum to display and publish the best of its Cypriot holdings in a more attractive form, not so much for their scientific value, but rather to promote his homeland, its archaeology and culture.

There are other non-scientific values placed on antiquities: for looters it is obviously just a matter of cash; for museums, a matter of prestige; for many, a simple enjoyment of their beauty; while for individual collectors it might be competitive acquisitiveness or perhaps pride in the personal ownership of a piece of ancestral heritage.

But for me it is the information value that matters, and all justified the countless hours in the darkroom, of chemical- and ink-stained fingers (that was then — I'd do it digitally, more cleanly and efficiently, now) and all the other work in compiling a big, but very dull book — one example of a species of publication threatened with extinction as museums increasingly make their collections available on-line, although many are far from convinced that this is a good substitute for our more traditional practices.

18
Water monkeys and wine

It's ANZAC Day. We're baking biscuits. The only time we ever use golden syrup, the 'cocky's joy' of the old pioneering days. As students in the late 1960s, we, too, relied on its cheap stickiness as we worked on our selection at Irrawang in the Hunter Valley.

Judy Birmingham — our quicksilver mentor and the project director — provided the academic legitimacy and dealt with official business. But much of the day-to-day work was organised by the Sydney University Archaeological Society — a communal exercise, appropriate to the times. We applied for funds from the Student Union, collected the few dollars a day each of us contributed, and did the general planning — who would be there when, and how they'd get there; organising the shopping (golden syrup always on the list); and put together all the bits and pieces needed in the field and in our camp — an abandoned service station on a by-passed section of the old Pacific Highway not far from the site.

Irrawang was also an abandoned place. It was a fairly short-lived affair, like so many other colonial ventures. Whatever their other failings, one must credit these settlers with enterprise and energy, albeit on stolen land. James King was one such entrepreneur, interested in all manner of manufactures. He'd experimented with raw materials for glass, then decided to move into wine, taking up land in the Hunter

18. Water monkeys and wine

IRRAWANG POTTERY WARE.
Consisting of filters mounted on stands, water goglets, 9d. each, porous monkeys, 2s. 6d. each, milk-pans, 14s. per dozen, ewer, basin, and chamber, for 2s. 6d., camp oven, bakers, 8d. each, wash basins, 8d each; mixing bowls, mugs, 3s. dozen; cullenders, 1s. each; butters, 1s. 6d. each; porous butters lined with glass, and wine coolers, ginger beer bottles, 18d. per dozen; preserving jars, pints, 4s., quarts, 6s. per dozen; jugs, from 6d. each; also, daily expected, pudding basins, pie dishes, and stone-covered jars.
Goods packed with care, and country orders punctually attended to, at
THOMAS R. COATES'S
Staffordshire Warehouse, 360, George-street, opposite the Markets.
N.B.—CRUCIBLES AND FLOWER POTS.

Valley in 1833. Alongside his vineyard he set up a pottery works ' ...*to manufacture only such coarse bulky articles as the mere price of the freight from England has hitherto excluded from the colony*'. He advertised a wide range of things: milk and cheese pans, cream and preserve jars, porous water monkeys (carafes to you!), colanders, filters, basins, baking dishes, bread pans, jugs and mugs, chamber utensils, ginger beer bottles and two-gallon stoneware wine jars which, filled with fine Irrawang wine, sold for 2s 6d.

A contemporary engraving gives an idealised impression of the business: a circular puddling-mill for working and mixing clay, sheds for forming pottery and drying it before firing in one

18. Water monkeys and wine

of several kilns, busily smoking away. A few workmen wander about, one with a load of pottery, another having a drink, perhaps sampling his boss's wine. An Aboriginal family watch on from the sidelines. I'd like to think that they represent Wonnarua people maintaining contact with their Country, but I fear they are just a standard stylistic convention.

Expert wine makers from Germany and potters from England were brought to Irrawang, for such skilled labour was in short supply in Australia then just as it is now. The wines they produced were highly regarded both locally and abroad, and the pottery sold well, despite intermittent hiccups in production.

But then it all changed. Not due to the usual business problems of economics, labour, quality, supply and demand, but the discovery of gold — a boon for a few, but a blow to many industries as workers ran off in the hope of making it rich. James King's vineyard and pottery suffered and effectively ceased production in 1851. The works were abandoned, buildings fell into decay and facilities were buried and overgrown with blackberry bushes, waiting for us to come along a little more than a century later.

Well, what was there to find? The most obvious feature was a clay-pit, although that clay proved too poor for most products and was mainly used for rough wares used in the production process.

18. Water monkeys and wine

Other features match those seen on the engraving, notably the circular puddling-mill and a nearby brick-lined mill for crushing clay preparatory to its sorting and mixing. And, of course, the kilns. All have elements of British pottery-making traditions, adjusted to suit the different, local conditions, and opening up questions of technology transfer and industrial adaptation in a new environment.

And, of course, there were lots and lots of fragments of pottery, some used by the workmen, but mostly bits of things broken during firing, as is common with all pottery-making. Most of James King's products were plain and utilitarian, mainly salt-glazed stonewares. But some lines were decorated with attached relief patterns and mouldings, using forms imported from England. People always like things to look nice!

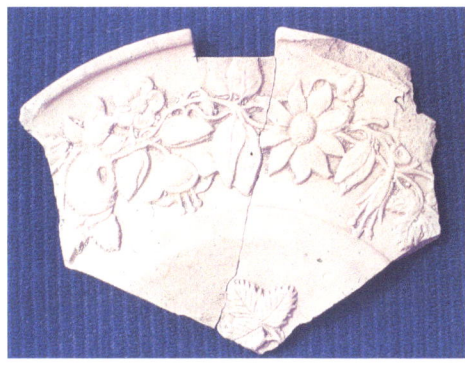
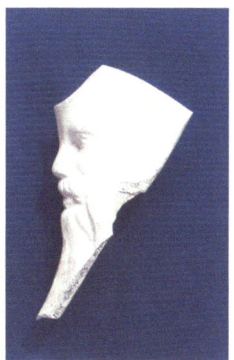

18. Water monkeys and wine

As always, excavation projects do more than just find stuff and contribute to knowledge, but also lead to further research and exploration. The work at Irrawang also provided a key stimulus to the development of historical archaeology in Australia, but for me and some of my fellow-students it gave a rare freedom no longer possible in our more managed and self-conscious times.

Nowadays our experiences, from initial project design to public exhibitions of the results, might be structured within formal courses, and framed by words such as 'hands-on learning' and 'job-ready training', but then we simply took this chance to play at being real archaeologists, to work on a complex site with features and structures and in doing so to develop logistical and practical skills. Each of our field seasons at Irrawang was something of a holiday excursion: serious, of course, hard-work, of course, but with a freedom no longer available, for there were few, if any, of the modern rules, regulations or health-and-safety protocols to bother us.

How lucky we were!

19
Significance

Modern housing estates sprawl around Melbourne. Those in Sunbury are typical of these neighbourhoods — there is even a Ramsay Court. Not far from it, just 250 mm away on the other side of Reservoir Road is Mumilam Korobine Nature Reserve, a  seemingly empty plot hemmed in by houses. Once, however, it was a focal point of highly charged activities. There Ancestors of Woi-wurrung speaking people carried out ceremonies in and around a circular ground they had prepared. Poorly preserved though it is, it is a significant place, one of only a small handful of surviving ceremonial grounds in Victoria.

I first saw some of these in 1978, less than a year after I'd returned to Australia, when Dan Witter persuaded me to investigate those in the grounds of the Salesian College at Rupertswood, once the estate of a powerful figure  in Victorian business and politics, W.J.T. Clarke, and known to the cricketing world as the home of the Ashes. On the other side of Sunbury from Mumilam Korobine, high on the slopes overlooking Jacksons Creek, three barely visible circular areas had been scraped out of the hillside, shallow circular features with slightly raised surrounding earth banks. What were they? Could they be Aboriginal constructions? If so, what were they? Or were they created by European settlers, invaders who destroyed

19. Significance

so much of Indigenous life and culture? And again, if so, what were they?

Now, had these rings been in northern New South Wales or Queensland there would have been no problem, for similar 'bora grounds' are common. But in Victoria they were not known to science and had no place on the Victoria Archaeological Survey register — hence Dan Witter's concern. And, to confuse the matter, we had the Volunteer Corps. For many years in the late nineteenth century hundreds of young men would take part in annual military exercises in what amounted to private armies. One camp was regularly organised by W.J.T. Clarke on his Rupertswood estate. These blokes did all sorts of things: perhaps they were responsible?

There is now an open view across the valley from the three rings but originally substantial trees hid both the view and the sites. They are unevenly spaced a few hundred metres apart, their low, partly eroded earth banks enclosing flat spaces some 15 to 25m in diameter. The one on the west is the smallest; the largest, on the east, has two concentric circular banks. Perhaps it was refurbished on different occasions. We carefully recorded all three, but I chose to excavate only within the central ring, where a group of scattered stones suggested some additional structure. We opened up a fairly generous area, to include a section of the bank and these stones. This proved to be a neatly made stone

19. Significance

cairn originally three or four courses (perhaps 30 to 40 cm) high. A second smaller cairn was found on the downslope edge of the ring. On this side the earth bank was formed by scraping back the thin soil down to the hard ground below; on the uphill side soil from both the interior and exterior was heaped up.

There was nothing to suggest military activity. But why should there be, and what would it look like anyway? But we did find many small chipped stone artefacts: a dozen small silcrete cores and small flakes struck from them, mainly clustered near the central cairn. Of course stone artefacts can be found almost everywhere, so, for the sceptic, even this does not definitely prove the earth feature itself was an Aboriginal construction.

Archaeology draws on any useful source to help solve its puzzles. Could other historical documents trump the suggestion of the Volunteer Regiment? Here we can turn to the limited accounts of local ceremonies recorded by interested Europeans even as their compatriots were destroying these vibrant cultures. The most relevant is that of Robert Mathews, who made notes on the initiation ceremonies described to him by Aboriginal men in the area of the Lodden, Campaspe and lower Goulburn rivers to the north of Sunbury. They explained that when there were enough young men of the right age, messengers were sent out to invite men from other groups to attend a ceremony. While they were away, the

> ... *whole of the men who remain at home select a suitable place for the meeting. In close proximity to the camp, a fairly level patch of ground is cleared of all rubbish and loose sticks, by collecting them into heaps and burning them off. The grass is then chipped off and the surface made smooth this space is enclosed by a circular bank of loose earth about six inches or a foot high and is called goanga.*
>
> *While waiting for the invited contingents to reach this general meeting ground, there are dances and other amusements, and ceremonial songs every evening. As each contingent arrives at the goanga, it is received in a formal manner by the hosts. The novices brought by each contingent, together with those who have previously*

19. Significance

> *arrived, are put into the goanga about dusk and kept there in company of some strangers for a short time.*

Mathews then described the long series of secret, often frightening events which took place over several days. At one stage the initiates had an upper incisor extracted, a common sign of initiation in this part of Australia. It is not hard to imagine such activities taking place in and around the Sunbury rings, for, as Mathews suggested, it is

> *... likely that the Yarra and Murray River people would attend each other's initiation ceremonies, and, although there would perhaps be differences of detail, most of their leading features would be similar.*

As for those stone tools we found — James Dawson, who had an intimate relationship with Indigenous people around Camperdown, explained that

> *... men and women are ornamented with cicatrices — which are made when they come of age — on the chest, back, and upper parts of the arms, but never on the neck or face. These cicatrices are of a darker hue than the skin, and vary in length from half an inch to an inch. They are arranged in lines and figures according to the taste or the custom of the tribe. The operator cuts through the skin with a flint knife, and rubs the wounds with green grass.*

Whatever else went on in this space, we can also imagine that older, senior men were producing those small sharp silcrete blades to be used in this way. While this is entirely possible, they certainly also scraped or cut up plants, wood, animals and birds, (or at least their feathers) perhaps for use in ceremonies. We now know this because of more recent and detailed specialist examination of the tools.

I'd handed over all my old field-notes and other documents on Sunbury to colleagues working with the Wurundjeri Woi-wurrung Elders as they developed plans for further research. I was happy to be able to do this — but for a while was more than a little worried about one thing: *where were the stone tools?* Had I just lost them? *Panic. . .* but then I thought that I might have — very properly — followed protocols of the time and deposited them in Museum Victoria, although I had no record and no

clear memory of doing so. Fortunately the Museum had acquired new storage facilities and staff had re-organised the archaeological collections, and so were very efficiently able to lay their hands on the artefacts, all carefully curated and accessible – crisis averted. *What a relief!*

In addition to the functional analysis, careful fitting together of many fragments showed how a Woi-wurrung speaking man struck off a series of small flakes from the core, once again part of the overall activities within the ring.

And, equally interesting, perhaps more importantly, new field-work located and re-opened the squares I'd excavated more than 40 years before. New techniques of luminescence dating of the sediments associated with the use of the ring show that it was constructed sometime between about 1,400 and 590 years ago — far older than I'd imagined and assumed.

While I was convinced that the rings were ancient ceremonial grounds and probably used for initiation ceremonies, others remained sceptical. But with these dates there is now no doubt that these places represent centuries, if not millennia, of repeated ceremonial activity by Woi-wurrung speaking Ancestors.

For many years I treated these earth rings as a puzzle, an academic exercise in archaeological and historical research, and often used them as an example in teaching

19. Significance

students about the problems of identification, explanation and the use of historical documents and analogies. I did not think that this, more than any other work I have ever done, would have the most value beyond the narrow confines of archaeology. This was strongly brought home to me years later when a Wurundjeri Woi-Wurrung Elder took over the explanation of their significance to my students when we met up at the sites. For him they were not an academic problem but were part of his cultural understanding of place and ancestral life.

As physical reminders of this core aspect of Aboriginal culture, these earth rings have a particular cultural value, well recognised by Wurundjeri Woi-wurrung Traditional Custodians Their future throws up many challenges. The three at Rupertswood and a fourth further up Jacksons Creek should — ideally will — become key nodes in preserving a broader cultural landscape, one that can recognise that these Aboriginal places were not isolated, enclosed sacred structures, but that the surrounding lands and setting were as important and significant as the ceremonial grounds themselves.

20
By the numbers

Skip this one if you are afraid of numbers or are naturally sceptical.

One thing (there are not many) that archaeologists agree on is that sherds are a bloody nuisance. There are just too many of them. And they are too demanding: needing cleaning, sorting, counting and, perhaps worst of all, storage, for no-one really knows what to do with the bags and boxes of seemingly useless waste — discarded in antiquity and no less unwanted in the present.

At Marki we'd dutifully collected and processed our fair share of pottery fragments. We sorted them into basic categories and counted the lot: 309,146 in total (see how long it takes you just to say all the numbers: *one, two, three . . .*). There is not much more you can do with most plain fragments, but a good-sized sample of

16,880 were given special treatment, with all manner of aspects of shape, texture, hardness, colour and suchlike things measured and documented. This gave us more than enough to play with. But, still, what to do with the bulk of our finds?

The devil, they say, finds work for idle hands. Not that ours were idle, but we thought we'd see if we could work out how many pots broke into that many pieces: it seemed a good idea at the time. Here we get very speculative, and there is plenty to be sceptical about as we used some creative accounting that, in

20. By the numbers

other circumstances, would surely land us in jail.

Let's start with how many sherds make a pot. Try dropping one on the floor and counting up the pieces. The first part of this had already been done for us by our Bronze Age Cypriots. We'd been lucky that one of our team had developed a special superpower as a pot-mender. Tim was able to sort through hundreds of almost identical fragments to pick out those which went together as parts of three-dimensional jigsaw puzzles each with an unknown number of oddly shaped, rough-edged pieces (with many missing). He'd then carefully build up the shape, sticking them together until magically he had repaired the whole vessel. Excellent!

All we then had to do was count the pieces in each mended pot and average out the number. Of course size and shape had something to do with this, but we came up with estimates of 23 sherds for big bowls, 12 for small, 59 for big jugs and similar types and 17 for small. So, if we divide the number of sherds in each category by these averages, we end up with 13,913 Red Polished ware vessels and 414 cooking pots.

That still seems like a lot of crockery. But remember that people lived there for about 400 years. How many pots per year? Easy: divide these numbers by 400. That is, 34 general vessels and 1 cooking pot per year of occupation. The small number of cooking pots is a bit of a surprise as we usually think of these as far more likely to break due to the stresses of heating, cooking and general use. But there it is.

We estimate that — again on average — there were about 10 families living in the area we excavated (sometimes fewer and sometimes many more). So only 3 or 4 pots would have been broken in each household each year. How does this compare with what happens in your house?

Now, this all assumes we'd found all the sherds from all the pots ever broken. Unlikely. Some would have been simply tossed away down the hill into the river; some would have been swept up with other garbage and dumped elsewhere; some perhaps collected along with animal droppings and human waste and carried off to spread out as manure in the fields (and in doing so creating ghost sites to confuse future archaeologists). So let's pretend we only found half the original number, we still end up with only about 7 or 8 pots per household per year.

We also need to remember that quite a few pots ended up in the cemeteries, placed (we don't know why) with each burial. In other places, such as Deneia, large tombs, reused over generations, accumulated scores, if not hundreds of vessels. But in the smaller tombs around Marki perhaps less than a dozen were provided for each person. We identified some 800 tombs in the cemeteries around Marki, conveniently found, emptied and left open by generations of looters. By some very creative accounting, it is possible to suggest that between about 3 and 5 people died each year. So, maybe we need to add another 30 or 50 pots to the annual needs of the whole community, not just those who lived in the area we excavated.

All this, however dodgy the numbers, is interesting — or at least I think so — for it opens up a discussion of where the pottery came from, who made it and where. Was it locally made? Were there specialist potters? When people first set themselves up in the new village with only two or three households manufactured goods such as pottery would have been brought in from larger, well-established places nearby. Perhaps later, when Marki village was bigger, there might have been sufficient local demand

20. By the numbers

to encourage someone to develop, maintain and practise the necessary skills in order to supply their neighbours with their modest annual replacements. Or perhaps, even then — as we later found at Ambelikou — there were more developed systems of production and distribution.

And then, at a more personal level, very rarely indeed, someone took the trouble to mend a broken pot. Unlike Tim, they had no glue, but a series of holes drilled along the broken edges allowed two halves of a  bowl to be laced together. It could not have been used for much, perhaps dry goods, nuts or fruit, but may well have been mended for the same reasons as Silas Marner, whose ... *'brown pot could never be of use to him any more, but he stuck the bits together and propped the ruin in its old place for a memorial'*.

21
Recycling Sotira

[Rabbi Yohanan] said to him: If I had not lifted up the potsherd, you would not have found the pearl underneath it.
Talmud Bavli, Bava Metzia 17b (translation by Rabbi Aidin Steinsaltz)

Blame this one on Covid. Like everyone else I needed something to pass the time during those long lockdowns, so especially harsh in Melbourne. With nothing better on offer I resurrected a long abandoned, indeed long forgotten, little project. It's a bit esoteric, rather technical and perhaps trivial. So feel free to give this one a miss.

Let's go back to prehistoric Cyprus.

'*The Sotira settlement was first noticed on the same day in February 1934 on which the Khirokitia site was discovered*'.

That's how Porphyrios Dikaios (you may remember him from other stories) introduced his substantial monograph on his excavations at Sotira Teppes. This site, set on the flat top of a conical hill overlooking the south coast of Cyprus, together with the more famous Khirokitia, provided him with the main building blocks for constructing what we now call the Cypriot Neolithic.

21. Recycling Sotira

Archaeology was very different then, and for Dikaios it was largely a bootstraps operation, for there was little else to go on, and much of that his own work. Radiocarbon dating which we now rely on was just being invented, so setting up a chronology was a difficult job. Sites and objects were generally placed into a series of successive cultures, stages in the evolution of society. This and other concepts, aims and questions framed how sites were approached and understood. Dikaios' view of Sotira was heavily influenced both by his discoveries at the larger, earlier site of Khirokitia and the way he saw finds as direct reflections of everyday life.

Dikaios and his team of skilled field-workers were well aware of the inherent difficulties of separating out meaningful layers and establishing their relationships to walls and other features. A key aspect was the identification of 'floors'. These are crucial to both his and our understanding of the site. I'm sure you appreciate that these were not nice, neatly laid floors with household items sitting happily on them. Rather they represent transitions within accumulated fill, where layers of harder mud, clay or other soil, as often as not patchy and uneven, could be traced across rooms. Things 'on' floors came from the soils accumulated immediately above these layers. There were often many items, almost all broken fragments of pottery together with chipped or ground stone, bone and antler. Underlying the floors thicker deposits incorporated an array of similar bits and pieces referred to as coming from 'between floors'. Dikaios then used the masses of information gathered over many months of excavation between 1947 and 1956 to build a history of the site, linking the layers within separate houses into four main Phases of building and rebuilding, sometimes occasioned by episodes of earthquake destruction.

Sir Mortimer Wheeler, who dominated British archaeology in the middle of last century, once wrote that 'all excavation is destruction'. And so it is. But it can also be seen as creation: the excavator carving out what will become the archaeological site from the accumulated sediments, structures and discarded rubbish. It is the privilege – and the responsibility – of excavators to present their creations to the world, framing the way in which

21. Recycling Sotira

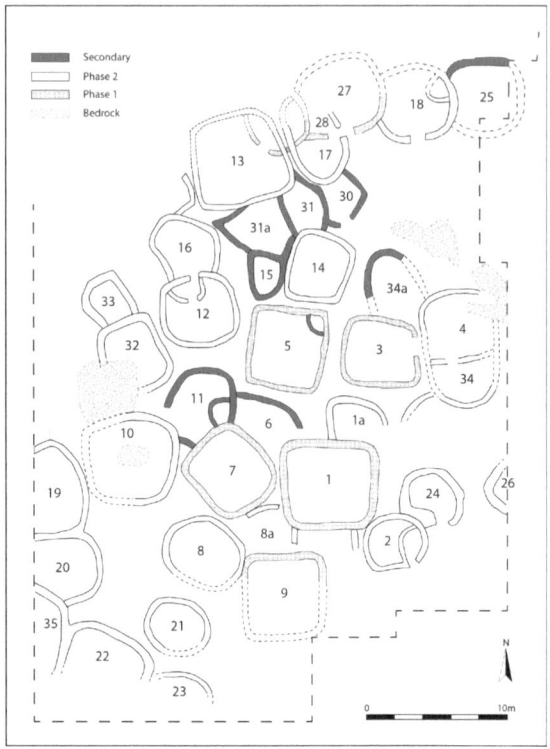

sites and the finds will be understood by future researchers. And to do so in a way that allows for alternative readings.

This applies to Sotira, where Dikaios' comprehensive site report successfully recycled the ruins and finds into a book – which then became, forever after, the site.

Fast forward a dozen years or so. A new generation were reconsidering the early prehistory of Cyprus and turned, naturally, to Dikaios' work. Eddie Peltenburg, excavating a site of the same period on the north coast of the island, looked for similarities and differences in structure and organisation of spaces and features. His Sotira looked a bit different from that of Dikaios. Meanwhile, Nicholas Stanley Price undertook a thorough analysis of the site as a whole, re-assessing the stratigraphic evidence and the grouping of layers, arguing for three rather than four Phases. Among other things he looked at the proportions of the different pottery wares in each Phase, concluding that there was no significant change

21. Recycling Sotira

during the life of the settlement.

In the early 1980s I'd used these contrasting studies in discussions of the nature of excavation, publication, analysis and re-analysis with my students. And, together with Caroline Bird, thought something different yet again could be attempted. We made a start, but what with one thing and another didn't follow it up: whatever notes and data we'd organised disappeared and neither of us can remember exactly what we thought we would do. And then, decades later, along came Covid and I pulled Dikaios' volume off the shelf.

I took Nicholas Stanley Price's chronological divisions – that is three rather than four Phases – as the starting point. But with a crucial difference. Nicholas based his calculations of proportions of pottery using all the sherds from each Phase. Influenced by a few decades of developing archaeological thought about the ways in which sites are formed and by my experience excavating the Bronze Age settlement at Marki, I felt there was likely to be a significant difference between the array of things Dikaios recorded as 'on floors' and those 'between floors'. It may seem obvious now but was not so in the past. At Marki we labelled some accumulations of things as 'use and abandonment' (more-or-less equivalent to Dikaios' 'on floors'). These assemblages of artefacts we felt were most likely to have been used and discarded toward the final use of a floor or building or immediately after it was abandoned. Other deposits could be far more mixed, incorporating stuff from different times: some old fragments might have been just lying about here and there while others would have been dug up from older deposits during construction works when houses were renovated or rebuilt. Perhaps this applied at Sotira. So I made sure to separate Dikaios 'on floors' from his 'between floors', as the latter was more likely to be a mixture of newer and much older material.

The mechanics of getting the data together is what passed at least some Covid-time. It was just a tedious matter of ploughing through Dikaios' site-report, counting up how many sherds of each pottery ware and many other things there were in each excavated context, and putting the information into a database: a task made more time-consuming by the way it had all been reported: comprehensive but not readily comprehensible, for Dikaios didn't go in for tables.

Anyway, at the end of this boring process I could play around with the numbers. Then we could see, for example, that there are indeed significant differences in the proportions of complete and broken stone tools found in fill and floor contexts. And where previously it seemed that there was no change in the proportions of the main pottery wares, the 'use and abandonment' or 'floor' assemblages show increases in Combed Ware and commensurate decreases in Red Lustrous Ware through time. The more muddled 'between floor' assemblages did not, of course, show this pattern of change. So, with a different way of organising the evidence we can now see that there was variation, even if it seems relatively minor, as fashions or something else affected what people wanted, made, acquired, used, broke, lost and discarded. And this raises of course a host of further questions...

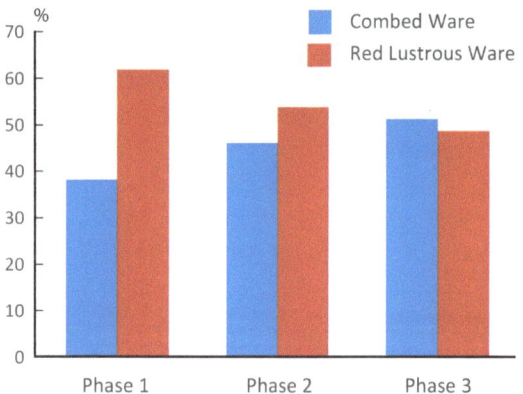

Trivial as it is, this is the stuff of archaeology – recycling old sites and transforming them into archaeological data; recycling that evidence into new products; and then again trying out yet further explorations of different facets of human behaviour and history. A never-ending story, but always so dependent on the work of our archaeological predecessors.

22
Questioning mounds

In the 1970s and '80s the university provided a range of student services, strange as that may now seem. Somehow the newish Division of Prehistory found a home among the medical practitioners. It was generally not a problem either for them or for us, although occasionally primal screaming therapy sessions next door disturbed classes, sometimes disconcertingly so if we happened to be discussing early hominid evolution and behaviour, especially in the late evenings.

Annette Berrryman was in the early stages of developing her postgraduate research project, and had become interested in Aboriginal mounds, a particular feature of areas along the central Murray River. One day, when passing the time with Rhys Lewis, one of the dentists who inhabited rooms beside our secretary's office – in those days academic departments had secretarial support, again strange as that may now seem – I happened to mention this. 'Well', said our friendly neighbour, 'you should come out to my bush block near Barham and have a look, for there are lots of mounds on it'.

Of course 'lots' is not a particularly precise number, and what do dentists know about Aboriginal mounds, anyway? But soon enough we were some 300 km north, having a look at the lightly wooded floodplain beside the Wakool River, an anabranch of the Edward River, which is, in turn, an anabranch of the Murray.

There were indeed mounds, and indeed lots of them, all different sizes, scattered across Rhys's block in among the big river red gums and the slighter black box trees. *Ideal!*

Although seemingly flat the floodplain had many subtle features. Apart from the main river channel itself there were lesser watercourses, hollows and depressions. Although a major waterway in itself, the Wakool would have followed the same pattern of annual spring increases in water flow, spilling out across the floodplains, and then gradually drying out again during the long, hot summer, with some isolated ponds and billabongs lasting longer than others. An initial, obvious question was whether there was a relationship between mounds and seasonally changing access and topographic context.

Annette had fruitful discussions of her project with members of the Wemba Wemba and Baraparapa communities, the Traditional Custodians of the Country whose ancestors created the sites and whose lives we were interested to explore; and we'd then got a permit to carry out fieldwork from New South Wales National Parks and Wildlife Service. So far, so good. But we were not entirely happy with the bureaucratic strictures they imposed: we were not to excavate holes larger than 1m^2. Now that is all well and good for many projects, places and research questions, but we'd hoped to look at the spatial structure of mounds and, obviously, you'd need to open up a larger area of one to do that. There was no persuading the heritage managers, so we had to accept their limitations and be happy with what we were allowed to do.

April and May 1982 saw our two field seasons. I was easily able to persuade a dozen or so students in my Australian archaeology class to spend their Easter break in the bush, starting the first phase of fieldwork: intensive survey in order to find and record all the mounds. We set up camp beside the Wakool River and got to work, systematically walking to and fro across all of Rhys's 250 ha block, plotting the location and describing the size and context of every mound we came across. By the end of a fortnight we'd found 95 mounds — certainly justifying Rhys's reference to 'lots'. Most were between 15m and 25m in diameter, the largest were generally on higher ground and spaced out along the bank of the main river channel, with smaller mounds near the minor watercourses, lesser channels, waterholes, depressions and wash pans.

By now you may well be asking *'what are these mounds?'*

22. Questioning mounds

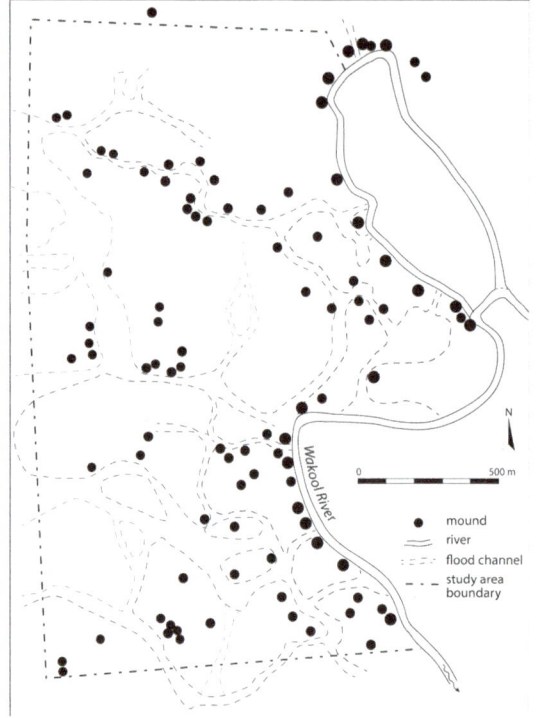
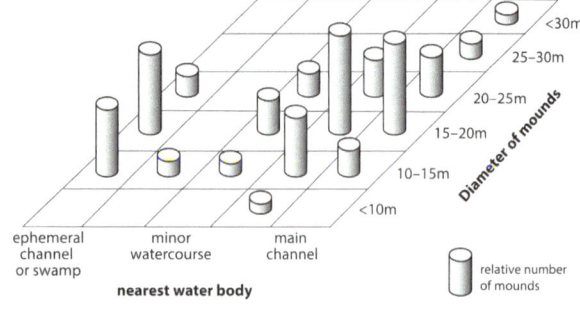

22. Questioning mounds

Perhaps the clearest account is by Peter Beveridge, who knew and wrote much about Aboriginal people along the Murray. In 1883 he discussed how mounds

'... *are essentially genuine cooking places, or cooking places and kitchen middens combined ... several of the* lyors *(women) go off with their yam sticks; when they reach the spot selected for the purpose, they begin with a will to excavate a hole about 3 feet in diameter and nearly 2 feet deep; during the digging of this hole any pieces of clay ... are placed carefully on one side with a view to their future use.*

When the hole has been dug sufficiently deep, it is swept or brushed out with some boughs or a bunch of grass; it is then filled to the top or a little above with firewood, which the lyors *have previously selected for that purpose. On top of the firewood the selected pieces of clay are then carefully placed, the wood is then ignited, and by the time it is all burned the clay nodules have become baked until they are exactly similar to irregular sections of well burnt brick ... the hot clay is removed from the hole ...* [food and hot clay balls are placed in the hole and covered].

When the cooking has been completed, the covering is scraped off, and the debris, consisting of calcined clay and burnt earth, becomes the nucleus of a black fellow's oven, such as are to be seen at the present day ... This process being repeated at short intervals, over a series of years, perhaps centuries results in the mounds ...

As a general rule the Aborigines do not erect the loondthals *(huts) on these cooking mounds; an exception to this exists, however on the extensive reedy plains of the lower rivers, which are annually inundated, remaining so for at least five months of the year.*'

A few weeks after our survey season we were back again, this time to excavate the small areas on and beside three mounds. While we found no stone or other tools, we could trace aspects of the way the mounds had been built up, much as described by Beveridge. Often enough we came across the baked clay heat-retainers, in one case a scatter of them, clearly left beside a

cooking pit once it had been opened and the food removed – just as they were left by some Aboriginal women many generations ago.

Radiocarbon and thermoluminescence dates indicate that this and the other two mounds that we tested began to develop sometime between about 3,500 and 2,500 years ago, more-or-less matching the dates from other excavations. Could there be earlier ones? Perhaps, for only a small number have been excavated, and older examples may have been covered by sediments deposited by the overflowing rivers. But it is also possible that there was a change to a new way of cooking in the relatively recent past.

As well as all the mounds we found 11 trees displaying the scars where bark had been removed. Bark taken from slighter species, such as box trees, may have been used for shields or dishes, while the majestic river red gums provided large slabs suitable for canoes — an essential part of Murray River peoples' tool-kit, used for travelling up, down and across rivers and access to inundated areas during periods of flooding.

Despite seasonal and other less regular variability, the riverlands were one of the richest areas of temperate Australia, well endowed with plentiful water, fish, plants, animals and waterbirds. Aboriginal populations here were, in consequence,

22. Questioning mounds

among the highest, and people stayed longer in particular places for longer periods than elsewhere. But all that came with some serious downsides, for population density brought with it a greater incidence of infectious diseases, and other adverse social and medical conditions.

But there are also some other intriguing possibilities, if we see the mounds as social features, and not only as evidence of cooking and so on. The larger mounds certainly stood out – easily recognisable, artificial features on the land. Did individual family or other groups recognise particular mounds as theirs? Did the spacing of larger mounds along the river bank represent a form of social spatial patterning and an avoidance of others' sites? In a time and area with denser populations, did mounds become – whether deliberately or accidentally – markers or symbols of ownership and identity?

23
Strike me pink

Colour is a tricky thing. It's an important part of any object, carrying with it aesthetic and symbolic meanings, constrained by traditions, techniques and the inherent nature of raw materials. But it is hard to define. Generations of archaeologists dealing with pottery have fallen back on descriptions like 'reddish-brown', 'creamy-white', 'pale yellow', 'buff' (whatever that is) and so on. We all know what these mean, more-or-less, when we are familiar with the vessels and fragments themselves. But they remain only somewhat vague and sometimes variable descriptions. Can we do better?

Here we can introduce Albert Henry Munsell, artist and professor of art. In 1905 he published *A Color Notation* setting out a formal system of defining colour in terms of three dimensions of hue, value and chroma (you don't really need to worry about what these are). After much fiddling about with techniques of printing and evolving research on how people perceive colour, a standardised set of colour charts was developed. These charts look a bit like those that you use to select what colour to paint your house, but instead of fanciful terms like 'belly fire', 'rusted crimson' and 'symphony red' you might have 10R3/2, 2.5YR5/2 or 7.5YR3/4.

Like all sorts of other scientists, a good many archaeologists got hold of copies of Munsell colour charts, especially the selection of soil colours, and began to use these in the field and for documenting pottery. Perhaps it helped remove some of the vagaries of less standardised terms. But few ever actually made use of the colours, other than for description. Many were suspicious of the reliability of data recorded in different light conditions by people with different quality eyes – really just questions of reliability and precision which could apply to all measurement. But it was also hard to see how to use them.

In my earlier work on Cypriot White Painted ware, I, too,

23. Strike me pink

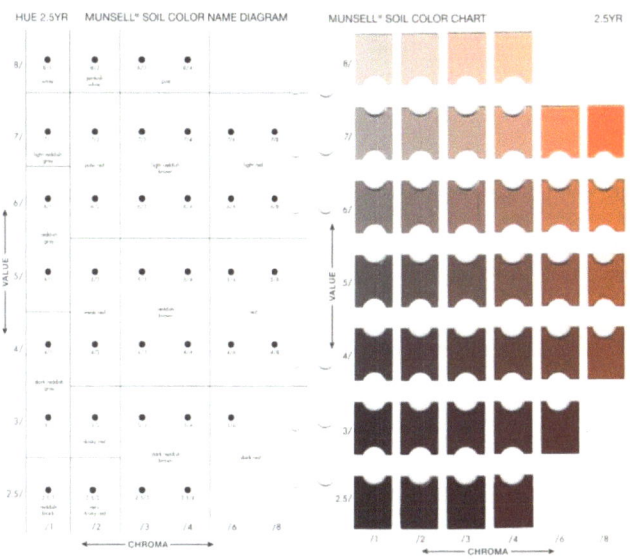

dutifully recorded the colours of hundreds and hundreds of pots in this way. My attempts to see pattern were not spectacular, but still more-or-less made sense, matching previously defined changes through time and, to some extent, space. Enough to encourage me to still record Munsell colours when we were excavating at Marki. And this we did, ending up with thousands upon thousands of records. And, fortunately, by this time they could all be entered into a data-base which allowed us to calculate the percentage of each recorded colour for each different type of pottery. And, again fortunately, some interesting patterns emerged. You can see them easily when plotted on an array of boxes each representing one of the relevant Munsell soil colour charts for hues from 10 Red to 10 Yellow-Red.

For example, we can compare the surface and fabric colours of Red Polished pottery, so-called because it is reddish and generally has a shiny, burnished surface. It was for some centuries the most common ware of the Cypriot Early and Middle

23. Strike me pink

Bronze Age. Here we will simply distinguish two varieties. Red Polished (Philia) — named after the village where it was first identified — is characteristic of the earliest phase of the Bronze Age. It should probably, by rights, be called Red Polished I, but the name was already taken by the time the Philia variety was found so it has this different name (see Stories 6, and 28). The other Red Polished ware considered here is from the next phase of the Bronze Age, developing from the Philia cultural system. This later variety we'll simply call Red Polished ware.

The surface colours are essentially the same: potters wanted to, and could, produce the desired reddish-brown surface with about the same consistency by selecting and preparing the ingredients of the covering slips so they had a greater quantity of iron and controlling the firing conditions. Here 2.5 Yellow-Red 5/4 and 2.5 Yellow-Red 5/6 make up over half the sample. Both earlier and later people wanted their pottery to be the same colour — a very long-lasting cultural preference.

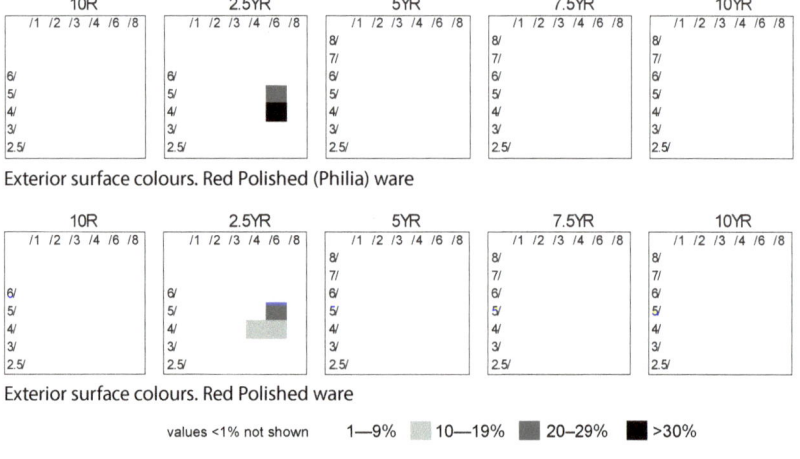

23. Strike me pink

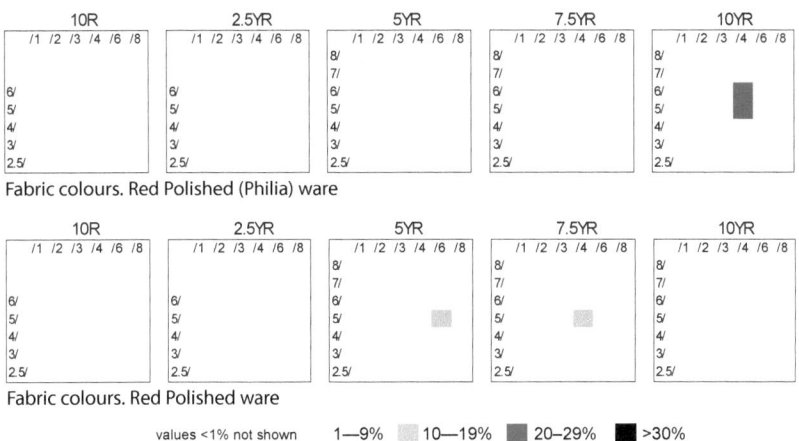

Fabric colours. Red Polished (Philia) ware

Fabric colours. Red Polished ware

values <1% not shown   1—9%   10—19%   20—29%   >30%

Now look at the fabric colours: the colours not seen, of course, when the pottery was in use, but reflecting qualities of the clay, not the added surface slip. There is relatively little consistency in the selection or preparation of the clays of the slightly later pottery. By contrast the Red Polished (Philia) fabric is far more uniform with over half either 10 Yellow-Red 6/4 or 10 Yellow-Red 5/4. These earlier potters were using more homogeneous clay sources. Perhaps you find this as interesting as I do.

Similar degrees of variability can be seen in other aspects of these two wares. Let's take hardness, for example. It is, again, a semi-subjective measure. But this time not so directly based on a universal system, such as that developed by Friedrich Moh about a century before Munsell did his thing. Moh ranked hardness of rocks and minerals on a 10-point scale with talc as the softest (1) and diamond the hardest (10). His scale has been widely used ever since by geologists and others, including archaeologists, but we found it easier to create a simpler scale of our own – soft, medium-soft, medium-hard, hard (there is other pottery that we scored as very soft or very hard, but there are none of those here). As you can see, the slightly later Red Polished ware is less consistent and tends to be somewhat harder than the more uniform Philia pottery, suggesting a difference in the clays used and perhaps also the way the pots were fired.

Far more sophisticated studies of the clays by a colleague, Maria Dikomitou-Eliadou, show that the Red Polished (Philia)

23. Strike me pink

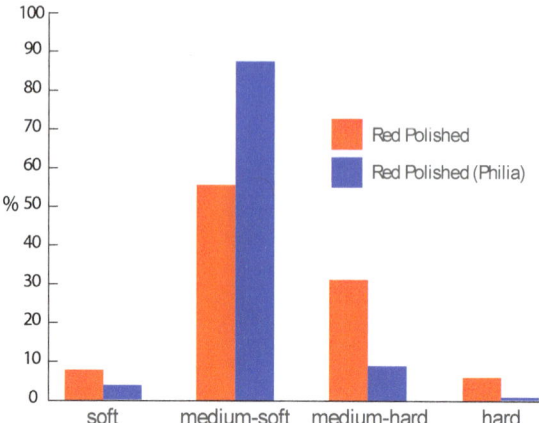

pottery was probably all produced in one particular region of Cyprus about 40km or so to the north-west of Marki and brought to our village when it was relatively new and small. Indeed, similar pottery was also sent all across the island, suggesting an integrated society, something supported by a range of other characteristic artefacts. Later Red Polished pottery was made in many different places, with more local production, not dominated by that one region. The variations in clay colour, hardness and other aspects of the fabric testify to this more diverse production. And also may equally be a symptom of a less cohesive, more divided population.

Perhaps you also find this as interesting as I do: I hope so.

24
Logistics

Sometimes the most important finds are not made in the field, museum or laboratory. Mr Polystipiotis' shop at 25B Trikoupi, a narrow side street in old Nicosia, was one such find. I don't know how we first stumbled upon
it, but visiting it became a highlight during preparations for the start of each field season, and often at other times.

Here we could find everything we wanted and much we had not realised we could not do without. For archaeologists need all manner of tools, utensils and gadgets, both outdoors and in, what with cubic metres of earth to shift and two to three dozen students to house and feed: balls of string and cord; buckets and basins; scrubbing-brushes, nail-brushes and tooth-brushes; sieves; torches and batteries; thermos flasks; pens and rulers; pencils, rubbers and sharpeners; cups, mugs and glasses; jugs, plates and bowls; knives, forks and spoons; pots and pans; clips and pegs; dust-pans and brushes and brooms — both modern household brooms and old-fashioned straw witch's brooms and the similar small straw hand-brushes or whisk-brooms, still the most efficient tool for sweeping on site – and how much sweeping we had to do! And the lists grew and grew.

But Mr Polystipiotis had it all, crowded into his narrow shop, the walls lined with shelves reaching far up to the high ceiling, for the old houses in Nicosia have high ceilings indeed. Each shelf and cupboard, drawer, tray and rack was crammed with stuff. If we couldn't see something we wanted, Mr Polystipiotis would know where to find it. He was a small man, quite stout, barely fitting between the shop counters and the walls, and no longer young, but he would happily scramble up his rickety ladder to reach

24. Logistics

across to the highest shelf and bring down whatever it might be, perhaps dislodging a shower of other oddments to be picked up and stuck somewhere in due course. If, by some remote chance, he couldn't find something, he'd scuttle around the corner to pick it up from a neighbour: we never left unsatisfied.

A significant find indeed.

25
To see oursels

*O wad some Pow'r the giftie gie us
To see oursels as others see us!
It wad frae monie a blunder free us
An' foolish notion:*

Robert Burns, *To a Louse*

Of course I should have known better.

But it was getting late, the winter sun had long set and the campus was dangerously dark – the end of a long day, bringing with it a little madness.

I had set my students the task of doing some research on artefacts from Papua New Guinea and to design museum displays. I like to think they enjoyed this challenge, combining theory and practice. Their displays were beginning to take shape – but there was a fly in the ointment. The artefact collections and museum space were shared with the sister discipline of anthropology, with all that this involves in the way of sibling rivalries.

My anthropological colleague had a very different view of both artefacts and

25. To see oursels

their displays. Mine was, I dare say, partly influenced by my time at the British Museum. He had less respect for the structured arrangement of things, focussed as he was on analysis of art, aesthetics, values and significance. Where we created areas to enhance the visitor experience (or some such high-sounding aim), he saw empty space as somewhere for him to teach, appropriately decorated with interesting and relevant objects.

So, he had brought in to our exhibition all the apparatus for lecturing: a clutter of chairs, lectern, an overhead projector and a slide projector on their stands and with associated screens. It was, you will appreciate, in the days before Powerpoint. Perhaps there was even a whiteboard: there were certainly trails of extension cords and other bits and bobs. Material culture. Just what archaeologists focus on and what museums are all about. What was more obvious than to treat all this stuff in the same way as the surrounding Melanesian artefacts? My students excitedly took up the idea and immediately set to work writing extra, increasingly extravagant labels and texts to explain the objects and their functions using the same terms and styles they'd used for the more exotic or ancient things. '*Kodak carousel slide projector, circa 1970*'; '*wooden chairs used by initiates*'; '*wooden stand used by the senior male to perform*'; '*pointed wooden staff, a symbol of status and authority*' . . . . you get the idea.

Eventually we all went home, happy with our work, both the original tasks and this crazy excursion, and imagining the reactions when the Anthropology class met the next day to find their things neatly labelled. And assuming, somewhat too naively, that they and my anthropological colleague would see the humour in it. And, more optimistically, would take up the opportunity it presented to engage in a critical debate on the ways in which we portray and explain different cultures: where our common, mundane material culture and its associated behaviour could be seen through the same gaze as that used for the exotic 'other' – to paraphrase Robert Burns' giftie, to see ourselves as we see others.

Oy, did I get a wrong number!
In Spades!

It was not long after that all archaeological involvement in that university museum came to an end.

26
Development

Running an excavation is more than a full-time job, but somehow Jenny Webb and I found time to revisit a small site a kilometre or two up the Alykos River from Marki. We'd seen it when we carried out a survey of the area before starting our excavations: a small field among the rugged hillocks of weathered volcanic rock, its surface littered with boulders from stone buildings and fragments of large pots and stone artefacts. We were far from the first to recognise Analiondas Palioklichia as a Late Bronze Age site – a large *pithos* (storage jar) came from there to the Cyprus Museum in 1936, and other pieces after that. But we felt it was worth another, closer look. I can't recall why.

It didn't take too much effort to count all the bits and pieces lying on the recently ploughed surface and to plot their location: it was certainly a lot easier than digging them up. All this stuff was concentrated toward the western side of the field, probably close to where it had originally been dumped or abandoned a little over 3,000 years ago. Most of the 200 or so stone artefacts were typical of those used for grinding grain. Almost all the hundreds of sherds were from large *pithoi*. These would have been quite sizeable vessels (think Ali Baba). There were next to no normal, more everyday domestic types of pottery. That was quite unusual. The

141

26. Development

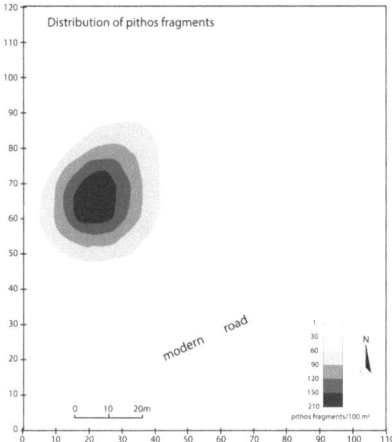
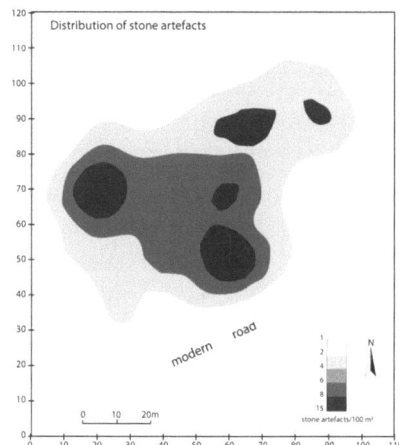

place, or what we could see of it, seems to have been used for storing commodities: grains, perhaps, or olive oil.

Among the *pithos* fragments one was of special interest. It had a scene in raised relief running along the shoulder – the impression made by a carved wooden cylinder rolled across the clay surface before the vessel was fired. The same scene appears on another fragment brought to the Museum in 1953 and it is very likely they come from the same vessel.

Our impression shows a full rotation of the roller. It is a hunting scene. The archer with his bow stands in his horse-drawn chariot while two attendants run behind. He is aiming at a bull, cow and calf, although, on our fragment, the animals appear behind the

hunters – the next turn of the roller would have placed them in greater danger in front.

Similar decorated relief bands on *pithoi* have been found at many other Late Bronze Age sites including the large coastal cities that developed in Cyprus at that time. The imagery is stylistically close to that common in the Aegean, the world of Mycenaeans and Minoans, and clearly represents activities of high-status people. These types of motifs were also used on small cylinder seals, widespread in the ancient Near East, their rolled impressions on clay or wax marking ownership of goods and to certify documents while serving, in themselves, as symbols of status, identity and authority.

For this was a far more complex society than in the villages of earlier times. Many of these, like our Early to Middle Bronze Age Marki, were abandoned as new social and economic systems and settlement patterns developed from about 1700 BCE. Older, less formal connections were replaced by tighter controls of inland territory and resources, with a series of competing kingdoms – or something of the sort — each with a dominant city with monumental public buildings, including temples and warehouses, such as Building X at Kalavasos where excavators found more than four dozen massive *pithoi,* each, on average, capable of holding about 670 litres of olive oil. That's a lot of oil. These were commercial as well as administrative and political centres, linked into the broader trading networks of the eastern Mediterranean during the Late Bronze Age. Cargo ships would have carried copper and other primary products from Cyprus to the surrounding mainland states, along with particular types of pottery, like distinctive small juglets containing opium or other precious substances.

So, what was this large, specially marked storage jar doing, along with all the other *pithoi,* at a small place in a very unprepossessing area, far from the centres of power?

If we look at the site in its setting we can make up a plausible story. Not many kilometres further upstream into the foothills of the Troodos Range are major sources of copper. Downstream, past our little village at Marki, is a Late Bronze Age fortified complex, and then further off across the plain is Enkomi, the

26. Development

earliest and largest city of the period. Archaeologists have developed ideas about the relationships between these different types of site, seeing them as parts of networks of control and distribution of goods. One suggestion is that there would also be others, including what we can think of as support villages, where agricultural goods and other things could be collected, stored and distributed to the miners. All forming a complex administrative system. A good idea in archaeological theory. Was our little site at Analiondas an actual example of one such place?

It certainly can be seen in this way. All those big storage jars, and not much else; the specially marked jar, with its iconic symbols of power impressed on it, perhaps the local administrator's special reserve; its location along a route to and from the mines in the hills.

The next step, obviously, would be to explore this idea further. Not immediately our business, for we had other interests to pursue. But perhaps a small excavation project could reveal its structure and, hopefully, confirm this interpretation. A small site, a neat project.

But, sadly, one never to be realised.

Within a few years of our work there no trace of the site remained. It doesn't take long for a bulldozer to reshape the landscape, levelling hills and flattening out terraces for agricultural installations. Such incremental, small-scale development, here as elsewhere on the island – indeed everywhere right across the world – is cumulatively destroying much of the archaeological record. It is these smaller, but none-the-less archaeologically important sites which can so easily disappear, often without ever have been identified.

So here one form of socio-economic development created this little site; another led to its abandonment about 3,200 years ago; and yet another to its total destruction within the last decades. I suppose there is a moral in there somewhere.

27
What you see is what you get

What fates impose, that men must needs abide;
It boots not to resist both wind and tide.
Henry VI, Part 3, Act 4 Scene 3

The first holiday house that Lena and I had at Cape Paterson was an old Californian bungalow that had retired there from an inner suburb of Melbourne. It was a somewhat sprawling place, more than a little rickety, never having quite recovered from the move. But it served us well. It also served as the base for introducing students to fieldwork in the mid-1980s.

For several weekends each year the house was full of them, sleeping wherever there was space in any and all the rooms. During the day Denise, Caroline, Rudy and I would divide them into groups and go out to walk along the beaches finding and documenting the evidence of past Aboriginal life in the dunes between the Cape and Kilcunda, some 20km to the northwest.

That part of the Victorian coast – traditional lands of the Bunurong people – has long stretches of beach, with occasional

27. What you see is what you get

low but steep cliffs. As one of the most southerly parts of the Australian mainland it is exposed to the south-westerly winds which seem to blow all too often. They can make life uncomfortable, especially when – again all too often – they are accompanied by rain and cold. But, when the sun is out, you wouldn't want to be anywhere else – as long as the flies leave you alone.

Over the years we surveyed, and re-surveyed, that 20 km stretch of the coast. Eventually we put all our varied notes together, and counted up 99 archaeological sites (that is what we called them then; now we would refer to them as 'Aboriginal, Ancestral, or Heritage places'). It would have been nice to have had a round 100, but what you see is what you get.

But what do you see, and what do you get?

Things are never as simple as we'd like them to be. Out along the beach those south-westerlies and heavier rains can move the sand around, sometimes eroding and exposing places and sometimes covering them up. You might see one larger place one year but three separate places the next. And then, when assiduous coastal land-managers plant sturdy grasses to trap and hold the sand, all the archaeological evidence may vanish, now deeply buried.

27. What you see is what you get

And that's not the half of it. *'99'*, you say? But where does one place end and another start? How far apart should exposures in the dunes be before we can be sure (*as if!*) that there is nothing under the sand between them? And then, what does an exposure of shells or stone artefacts represent? – one visit to that place or the remains of things discarded on several occasions?

Too hard! Or is it really a matter of asking the right questions of this fickle evidence,

Rather than looking at, or for, specific details, precise numbers and so on, we need to think about the overall structure of the evidence. None of our '99' places seems to have been very substantial. Most have shells, but a number only had stone artefacts: perhaps they never did, although it is also possible that any associated shells have disintegrated, the fragments blown or washed away. In particular spots, such near the estuary at the mouth of the Powlett River, the middens are more obvious and may have been larger than most. But, in the main, we have a light and relatively even scattering of evidence all along the coast. No particular areas seems to have been preferred or the repeated focus of activity, perhaps because the rock platforms and their resident shellfish were fairly evenly distributed. Nor did people always favour any one particular species of shellfish, but collected what was available at the time.

Looking at this as an archaeologist, I'd suggest that this shows a lack interest in the coast and its resources by Bunurong Ancestors. But my friend Adam Magennis tells me something different – that his mob are saltwater people, and continue to view shell middens as important cultural monuments marking Bunurong places along the coast. Certainly, when time, tide and weather were convenient, people would go out onto the rock-platforms to collect shellfish and to dive to pick up larger animals from the lower tidal range. And then to sit up on the dunes to eat their catch. Here too, people sometimes fashioned and used

27. What you see is what you get

stone tools, either bringing good quality stone with them, but more often collecting flint washed up on the beach from outcrops far out under the sea. At the same time there was a major focus away from the beach, around the low-lying wetlands behind the dunes,  or further inland across the coastal plain and even up into the South Gippsland hills, then densely covered by the tall trees of the temperate rain-forest.

Now I have to warn you we have precious little evidence for what I've just said. If shell-middens have their problems, finding scatters of stone tools in the well-vegetated grasslands is even more difficult. But we know that people were there and will eventually, if gradually, know more of how they lived. Meanwhile, both those sites we now know about and those which we don't are precious Bunurong heritage, whatever their archaeological problems.

28
Hunting a solution

Bernard was quite persuasive. But Jenny Webb and I didn't need that much convincing, especially as we'd be happy to go back to a settlement after being so rudely rejected by the cemeteries at Deneia (Story 2). Among the many sites found in the northern foothills of the Troodos Range during his Sydney Cyprus Survey Project was one that Bernard called Politiko Phournia. One of his teams had carefully documented it, collected a sample of the surface sherds and used a geophysical technique to look below the surface. The resulting murky, blotchy picture, could, like Hamlet's cloud, be whatever you wanted; Mr Rorschach, too, would have been interested. By squinting a little, about ten fuzzy circular somethings could be made out, maybe. Once neat lines were drawn onto them they certainly stood out of the murk, for all the world like the buried stone footings of ancient walls of separate structures. The pottery was also a bit murky but appeared to be what could be described as '... an intriguing Late Chalcolithic, perhaps, with Middle Chalcolithic undertones and a tantalising hint of Early Bronze Age'.

If you read the next story or remember Story 6 you'll understand why this last aspect attracted us, for the relationships between the indigenous Chalcolithic people of Cyprus and the

28. Hunting a solution

incoming Bronze Age settlers about 2,400 BCE was – and still is – an important and challenging question.

So we thought it worth a go. Preliminary small tests at Fournia (we used this alternative spelling following modern official style) didn't help much but didn't put us off. Neither did a new geophysical survey which didn't show anything at all, not even the weakest suggestion of any buried features.

There we were in the spring of 2008 with our team of students ready to work at Politiko Kokkinorotsos (by this time we'd changed its name again. Not just the spelling, but because it was really within the locality of Kokkinorotsos, and not nearby Fournia). We were all geared up to excavate a Late – hopefully final – Chalcolithic village with evidence of interaction with new Bronze Age neighbours. The village we expected to be something like those on the south coast of the island, with substantial circular houses. But we found nothing of the sort. Nor, indeed, any trace of the Early Bronze Age at all.

What did we find as we cleared a very large area of the shallow ploughsoil off to harder surface below? No stone features, no houses, nothing very clear, just some odd-shaped hollows

28. Hunting a solution

or pits (but not where the original geophysics suggested something) and one larger, natural depression. Could these features be some type of structure? There were none of the post-holes you'd expect if there were huts, shades,  shelters or tents. Some scattered lumps of harder clay may have been from packed earth used in construction, but that didn't help much. There was a possible hearth and – we think – an earth oven for cooking large quantities of food. But there was no pattern to anything. Disappointing, yes; frustrating, very.

The old surface was littered with bits of pottery and stone artefacts, the hollows, pits and depressions filled with much, much more: over a tonne of pottery fragments, along with many stone tools and tonnes of animal bones (well, perhaps not literally tonnes in this case, but over 7,000 pieces). This was not the normal casual refuse from daily living, but the deliberate dumping and disposal of garbage originally discarded somewhere nearby. So, with a little help from some friends, our attention turned toward all these finds to make sense of the site.

28. Hunting a solution

First the pottery. It was all very broken up: fragments of different shaped vessels, some plain, some painted and of finer quality than others and some with tubular spouts, clearly for pouring liquids. Pity poor Tim, desperately trying to find pieces that would join and to mend up whole vessels. But it was all just too jumbled up, and nothing came easily together. So we had no complete shapes to compare with other places. But it was certainly not Late Chalcolithic, nor was there any sign at all of the Early Bronze Age. Instead there were several varieties of what fitted best with the Middle Chalcolithic pottery traditions known elsewhere. The relatively minor differences could easily be explained by regional variation, for this period was otherwise unknown in the centre of the island.

And the radiocarbon dates fitted well, with 12 samples returning almost identical ages, showing the place was used for a while between 2880 and 2670 BCE. There is precious little evidence of that age anywhere on the island – a transitional and little understood time between the Middle and Late Chalcolithic, as murky as those geophysical plots.

Next, the stone artefacts. We were lucky that Carole McCartney was happy to study the chipped stone tools for us, for this was her special expertise. She showed that the tools fell into three main groups, all associated with processing animals: scrapers with the use-polish and use-damage from cleaning and scraping hides; wedges and tools with sharp points for splitting and cutting grooves into bone, perhaps to extract the marrow. The ground stone – pounders, grinders and the like – were mostly those for processing wild food, such as fruits and nuts, with very few of the axes, adzes and other tools used for woodworking commonly found at other Chalcolithic sites.

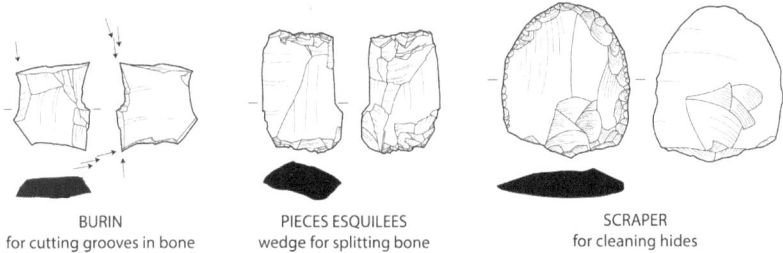

BURIN
for cutting grooves in bone

PIECES ESQUILEES
wedge for splitting bone

SCRAPER
for cleaning hides

And, finally, all that animal bone. Once again we had special help. For many years Paul Croft has been the go-to man for studying animal bones in Cyprus. He'd 'done' the bones for us at Marki and at many other sites and was intimately familiar with the

Chalcolithic animals of the south coast. He has handled more of them than anyone else ever has, or probably ever will. He came to help us at the site, bringing welcome expertise to its challenges, but was as frustrated as we were by its lack of clarity. Later he spent weeks and months going through the bones. An interesting result. Nearly three-quarters of the bone was from fallow deer – a species introduced to Cyprus long before but at this time feral. Almost all the rest were goats and sheep – again not domesticated sheep, but the wild mouflon. There was also a dog and a few stray pigs, hardly worth mentioning.

But it was mainly deer.

Because the deer were never a domesticated species, this must represent hunting. Paul also noted that the body parts and the ages at which the sheep and goats were killed were characteristic of hunting rather than managed domestic herds. This opens up – at least for those interested in such things – the question of seasonality. Several lines of evidence indicate that hunting took place in the warmer months. The first is the absence of male sheep over three years of age. In the summer older males separate from the females and younger animals, which can be more easily hunted at this time of year. There were also not a few foetal and neonatal bones, indicating late winter and early spring kills of pregnant ewes and little lambs.

Further studies confirmed Paul's observations. Once again we could draw on specialist help, in this case from Anne Pike-Tay. We knew her because she'd worked with colleagues at our university on ancient wallabies from Tasmanian sites, although deer are more her thing. She has developed techniques for studying the annual growth patterns of animal teeth, and we were able

28. Hunting a solution

to get permission to send some of our teeth from Cyprus to her in America. Anne used these to show that both fallow deer and mouflon were hunted and killed between late winter and late summer.

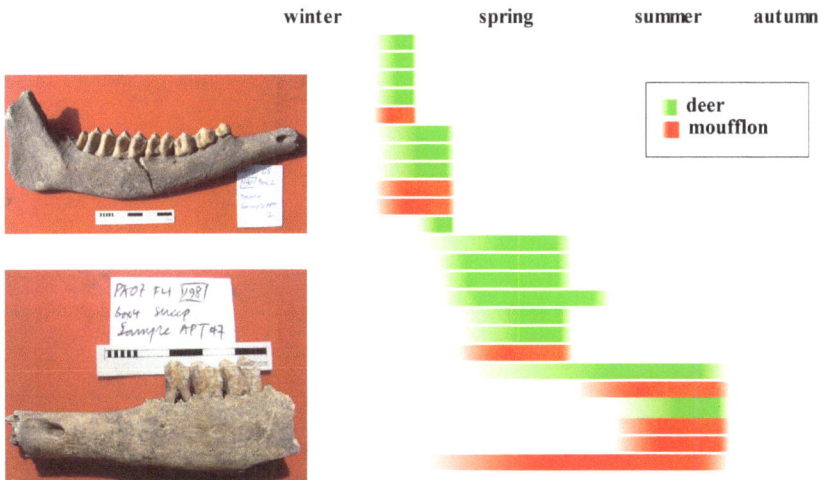

So – what do we have? The limited extent of occupation, the absence of substantial structures and burials, the lack of agricultural and timberworking tools and the spring and summer exploitation of animals suggest that Kokkinorotsos was not permanently occupied, but only used in the warmer months. Hunting was the main activity, along with processing the meat, hides and bones. But other things also went on at the site. Storage vessels, spouted jars and bowls and fine ware eating and drinking vessels, as well as domesticated cereals and cereal grinding equipment, together with the earth-oven point not only to everyday eating and drinking, but perhaps also special feasting.

In the end, instead of what we'd wanted to find, we exposed a new and different type of site – a special-purpose, seasonal hunters' camp. It must have been one part of a broader economic and settlement system involving permanently occupied farming villages and seasonally used outstations. Once again new information and new prospects emerge when least expected, creating new challenges to explore additional complexities in ancient worlds.

29
Back Stories

Looking forward, looking back
I've come a long way down the track
Got a long way left to go
Making songs, from what I know.
Slim Dusty, lyrics by Don Walker

When he offered me a scholarship to come to Gothenburg in 1973 Paul Åström saw this as closing a circle: 27 years earlier he had travelled to Australia while working on his doctorate to stay with Eve and Jim Stewart at the ancestral Stewart mansion near Bathurst. Paul's thesis on the Middle Bronze Age was later published as *The Swedish Cyprus Expedition Volume IV 1B*. Stewart's posthumous contribution to that series was the second half of *Volume IV 1A,* on the Early Bronze Age. In the years leading up to his death in 1962 Stewart became increasingly grumpy because, despite its 290 pages and 1438 drawings of pots, his half of that book had to be restricted to not much more than an outline of his massive compilation and intricate classification. You can sympathise with the editor, Einar Gjerstad, far away in Lund, his patience tested by the Australian author's demands and delays. And not only that. He also found himself cast in   the role of referee in an academic stoush between Stewart and Porphyrios Dikaios, who dealt with the earlier periods in the first half of *The Swedish Cyprus Expedition IV 1A*. It was all about the

29. Back stories

end of the Stone Age and the beginning of the Bronze Age, something touched on in Stories 6 and 23.

It was a bit like digging a tunnel from both ends and failing to meet in the middle. Alongside Stewart's obsessive, controlling personality, the rigid structures of the entrenched formal Ages and Periods contributed to this misalignment. And, truth be told, still get in the way of many archaeologists' thinking.

To understand this fully you must forgive a little detour, still with a Scandinavian connection, into much earlier archaeological history. Nearly 200 years ago Christian Thomsen, followed by Jens Worsaae, developed the Three Age System. You've all grown up with it, and it is deeply embedded in your brain, even if you've never heard the term. Sorting out the collections in the National Museum of Denmark, they demonstrated an archaeological sequence of Stone, Bronze and Iron Ages, something we all take so much for granted that we seldom ask where this concept came from. A generation later Oscar Montelius (a Swede this time) came to the party, again using changes in associated sets of objects to subdivide the Three Ages in Scandinavia into finer periods. Soon everyone in Europe was talking in terms of the Early, Middle and Late Bronze Ages, and then discovering, perhaps inventing, ever finer subdivisions, labelling them as I, II, III and so on and on and on.

The infection spread to Cyprus.

When the British did a deal with the Ottoman Empire and took over the island in 1878 their archaeologists were quick to take advantage of access to what they saw as their own piece of the Mediterranean world: they wouldn't have to put up with interfering locals any more. Soon Sir John Myres and Max Ohnefalsch-Richter corralled pottery from ancient tombs into the fashionable Early, Middle and Late Bronze Ages. Nothing wrong with that.

The next plot twist re-introduces a Swedish connection.

March 1922. A train station in Serbia. Professor Axel Persson is on his way to his excavations in Greece. A mysterious stranger approaches. 'I am Luke Pierides', he says, and on learning what Axel Persson is doing, says he, too, is passionate about archaeology. And on learning Axel is Swedish, he claims to be the Swedish Consul in Cyprus. Later he explains that the Serbian police took all his money. Could he borrow some? A doubtful but sympathetic Axel hands over £5, and later another £5, not expecting to see any of it again. But, surprisingly, it is all true. Luke Pierides was indeed the Swedish Consul in Cyprus, a member of an important Cypriot family with a long history of interest in antiquities. He then encouraged Axel to send out a bright young student to study the archaeology of Cyprus. And so, in 1923, Einar Gjerstad arrived on the island.

By 1926 when he published his PhD thesis, Gjerstad had studied the Bronze Age material in the Cyprus Museum and had carried out excavations at three settlement sites, a necessary complement to all the old finds from tombs. He separated out varieties of pottery so that he could subdivide each of the main Bronze Age periods into three – I, II, III. Just like everywhere else.

Einar was so taken with Cyprus that he set about organising what became the Swedish Cyprus Expedition. Together with three of his mates (and their wives) they spent several years on Cyprus. Between 1927 and 1931 they moved around the island, setting up camp and excavating at one site after another. Even after the antiquities authorities took their share, dozens and dozens of crates of finds were shipped off to Stockholm.

Efficient as always, within six years Gjerstad and his team were able to publish very substantial reports on the 19 sites that they had excavated as *The Swedish Cyprus Expedition Volumes I, II* and *III,* each dealing with a different period. The final, summary *Volume IV*, took far longer to appear – and had to be subdivided (you guessed it) into three, again each dealing with a different period. Even then *Part I* (The Stone Age and the Bronze Age) had to be divided yet again – this time, eventually, into four), with *IV 1A* uncomfortably shared by Dikaios and Stewart. And that's where our clash of these Titans erupted, with Gjerstad in the middle.

29. Back stories

You now understand the Swedish connection, while Dikaios' involvement in the past of his island home needs no special explanation. But Australia? Of all places?

The first connection was inauspicious. In 1890 an added note in the field report of the British Cyprus Exploration Fund in the *Journal of Hellenic Studies* explained that,

> 'Mr. Tubbs having left England early this year to take a post in Australia, the task of seeing his work through the press has devolved on others . . .'.

Unfortunately the subsequent history of Henry Arnold Tubbs (later Talbot-Tubbs) in Australia and New Zealand was not a happy one, but that is another story which has nothing to do with Cyprus.

We need to skip forward 40 years or so to meet Jim Stewart, who has appeared in several stories already. By all accounts he was also not an easy man, although somewhere on a different spectrum from Henry Talbot-Tubbs. Born in Australia but largely educated in England, he read archaeology at Cambridge. In 1937–1938, prompted by an interest in connections between southeastern Turkey and Cyprus, he excavated at the Early Bronze Age cemeteries at Bellapais Vounous, where Dikaios had previously worked. Publication of the excavations was delayed by the war, especially as Stewart was captured in Crete while serving with the Cyprus Regiment. He was able, however, to continue with some research while a POW (some of his books which I used in the Fisher Library at Sydney University in the 1970s were inscribed *Oflag VIIB*). The field report on Vounous was published by the Swedish Institute in Rome in 1950 through the efforts of Einar Gjerstad (it's a small world!). Stewart saw this as a precursor to a comprehensive compilation of everything about the Early Bronze Age which he hoped would to come out as a volume of the *Swedish Cyprus Expedition*. Gjerstad may initially have gone along with this notion but would have had no idea of the massive scale of the project, something which occupied Stewart for the rest of his life. After he died in 1962 his widow, Eve, spent another 40 years in an attempt to realise his vision. Only after her death was it finally completed when Jenny Webb and I edited the fourth volume in 2012 — by which time, of course, new evidence and changing attitudes, approaches and techniques made it almost entirely redundant.

Back to where we started. That divide between the Ages.

What happened was that during the war years Dikaois carried out rescue excavations near Philia Village. The tombs contained pottery which was clearly like that of the well-established Early Bronze Age Red Polished ware but differed in shape and in other ways (look again at stories 6 and 23). Dikaios, comfortable with the ordered concepts of sequences of Ages and Cultures saw this variety as early, preceding Early Cypriot I. But what comes before 'I'? In his half of the *Swedish Cyprus Expedition Volume IV 1A* he opted for 'Initial Stage of Early Cypriote I'. Moreover, he felt that the differences between this material and the Chalcolithic, the Age preceding the Bronze Age, and which he knew better than

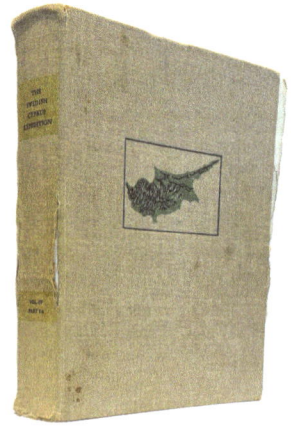

anyone else, were so great that this 'culture' must represent the arrival of new people, Bronze Age migrants to the island from Anatolia (ie modern Turkey).

Stewart wasn't happy. Perhaps he was also a bit miffed that he'd seen 'Philia' type things at Vasilia on the north coast in 1937 but he hadn't done anything about them and had missed the opportunity to work them into his system. He just didn't like the idea of a new period (Dikaios' 'Initial Stage') at all. He preferred to see these 'Philia' pots as a regional variation of Early Cypriot I. He also didn't approve of the idea of an Anatolian origin. And anyway, he was the one in charge of the Early Bronze Age and wasn't going to allow anyone else to tell him what to do with it or with Red Polished pottery (even Paul Åström wasn't able to include all the Middle Bronze Age Red Polished pottery in his thesis).

So, the issue was left unresolved: Gjerstad had to settle for a schizophrenic *Volume IV 1A* with two ways of seeing and presenting the evidence and two ways of understanding the history.

Of course archaeology doesn't stand still. Philia pottery and other objects began to be found beyond the regional area Stewart had sketched out, as far away as the south coast of the island. *Dikaios 1, Stewart 0.*

And then we found clear stratigraphic evidence at Marki, with Philia material below, and so earlier than, the normative Early Cypriot I–II phases of the settlement. *Dikaios 2, Stewart 0.*

We hadn't expected to find this evidence or anything of this period, and had no previous interest in stepping into this old debate. But now we had to. The more we looked at the differences between the preceding Chalcolithic and the Philia Bronze Age material the clearer it became to us that Dikaios must again be right. What we saw was a whole suite of new technologies and ways of life, from metallurgy to farming, from pottery making to cooking and even in the way in which babies were held. This was not an internal evolution from one time and cultural system to the other. Instead it we felt that it must represent Anatolian migrants bringing their Bronze Age to Cyprus. *Dikaios 3, Stewart 0.*

Questions and ideas like these are always clouded by an easy confusion of 'Ages' with 'Cultures'. Basically, the archaeological evidence represents a sequence of developments, of change through time, even if the evidence often has to be squeezed into long established, even outdated, frameworks of defined periods. But material differences have also come to be seen as markers of different peoples, ethnic groups or cultures, problematic concepts in themselves. This way of thinking fell out of favour in archaeological explanation in the second half of last century, and, along with it, the associated arguments for migrations of peoples — for if these could not be identified, how could one argue for their existence, let alone movements?

Nevertheless we felt the nature and timing of the Philia Bronze Age material could best be explained by the incursion of a new group into the island. This opens up a new, and exciting, set of issues. For Dikaios, the transition from Chalcolithic to Bronze Age was rapid, the replacement of one group by another, fitting with a model of neat, defined Ages, and hence Cultures. We can now suggest that there was a much longer time when the new settlers and the older indigenous peoples co-existed on the island. How long? That we just don't know: there is simply not enough (really hardly any) evidence. But soon enough (several generations, maybe) we cannot see any obvious trace of Chalcolithic material culture: everywhere it is just Bronze Age. *Materially* Bronze Age. We must, however, imagine that in some villages and places people still thought, prayed, spoke and danced in their old tradition, retaining a distinct feeling of identity, even if they now looked, archaeologically, like everyone else on the island. Now we need to re-frame our questions from history to process, and to consider the nature of the cultural and social interactions and relationships between these two groups and the effects of each upon the other. *Much more interesting!*

This will be a challenge for future archaeologists: to find the evidence and develop new histories and understandings of the past and to escape the shackles of outdated attitudes. But in doing so they will still need to balance their insights with an appreciation of earlier research. For there are always more back stories, of the distant past and of those who explored it. One day we will all be characters of the past: but will we be as interesting to our successors as those who came before us?

30
Not an afterthought

R. Hanina said: 'I have learned much from my teachers, and even more from my colleagues, but most of all from my students.'
Talmud Bavli, Ta'anit 7a

To Rabbi Hanina's well known list I can add 'and also from the places I have excavated', for they are all different and, as seen in these stories, each site has its own character and can produce unexpected tricks and challenges. There is always the need to learn from and to respond creatively to their demands – as well as to the ever-changing landscape of techniques, methods and theory.

For me this lifetime of learning began in 1967 when I was lucky enough to work on excavations as different as a Maori pā in New Zealand and a rockshelter in New South Wales – and, as a volunteer with the Department of Antiquities, an array of ancient places in Israel. And, at the same time, to learn from the excavators,

30. Not an afterthought

all equally different in approach and style – as well as attitude and personality.

While neither they nor their excavations feature much in this book, it is appropriate to end it with a brief, inadequate, mention of some those from whom I learnt in the field in those early years: Jack Golson and Wal Ambrose at Kauri Point; Ron Lampert at Burrill Lake; Judy Birmingham at Irrawang, Wybalenna and Zagora; Basil Hennessy and Tony McNicholl at Teleilat Ghassul.

Read more about it

Research publications require the inclusion and at least the symbolic support of references to primary sources of fact, opinion and theory. The few studies listed here should reassure readers that there is some substance to the archaeological aspects of these stories and give anyone sufficiently excited an idea of where to go for more details or to start on the mountains of related literature.

1. The truth of the matter

Edmond Sollberger, 'The White Obelisk'. *Iraq* 36 (1974) pp. 231–238.

Julian Reade, 'Aššurnasirpal I and the White Obelisk'. *Iraq* 37 (1975) pp. 129–150.

Julian Reade, *Assyrian Sculpture*. British Museum Press, London (1999).

2. No Sleeping Beauty, this

David Frankel and Jennifer Webb, *The Bronze Age Cemeteries at Deneia in Cyprus*. Studies in Mediterranean Archaeology CXXXV. Sävedalen (2007). [associated digital archive http://library.latrobe.edu.au/record=b2234894].

David Frankel, *A Thousand and One Tombs: Survey, Sampling and Ceramics in Bronze Age Cyprus*. The Twelfth Museum of Antiquities Maurice Kelly Lecture, University of New England, Armidale (2008).

Jennifer Webb and David Frankel, 'Exploiting a damaged and diminishing resource: survey, sampling and society at Bronze Age Deneia in Cyprus'. *Antiquity* 83 (2009) pp. 54–68.

3. Spirits of times past

David Frankel and James Rhoads (eds), *Archaeology of a Coastal Exchange System: Sites and Ceramics in the Gulf of Papua*. Research Papers in Archaeology and Natural History No. 25. Division of Archaeology and Natural History, Research School of Pacific Studies, Australian National University, Canberra (1994).

Australian Museum, *Frank Hurley in Papua.* https://artsandculture.google.com/story/frank-hurley-in-papua-australian-museum-sydney/MAWB56LwVqwZJw?hl=en.

Frank Hurley, *Pearls and Savages*. G.P Putnam's, New York and London (1924).

Read more about it

4. Mary-Ann and the seafarer
James Stewart, 'The Tomb of the Seafarer at Karmi'. *Opuscula Atheniensia* 4 (1962) pp. 197–204.
Jennifer Webb, David Frankel, Kathryn Eriksson and Basil Hennessy, *The Bronze Age Cemeteries at Karmi Palealona and Lapatsa in Cyprus. Excavations by J.R.B. Stewart.* Studies in Mediterranean Archaeology CXXXVI, Sävedalen (2009).
David Frankel, 2013. 'Recovering two ancient sites in Cyprus'. *Humanities Australia* 4 (2013) pp. 74–83.

5. A Spirit Board
Frank Hurley, *Pearls and Savages.* G.P. Putnam's, London (1924).
Robert Welsch, Virginia-Lee Webb and Sebastian Haraha, *Coaxing the Spirits to Dance. Art and Society in the Papuan Gulf of New Guinea.* Hood Museum of Art, Metropolitan Museum of Art, New York (2006).
David Frankel, 'Carving a gope board'. *The Artefact* 33 (2010) pp. 49–55.

6. An embarrasment of bronze
Jennifer Webb, David Frankel, Sophia Stos and Noel Gale, 'Early Bronze Age metal trade in the Eastern Mediterranean. New compositional and lead isotope evidence from Cyprus'. *Oxford Journal of Archaeology* 25 (2006) pp. 261–288.
David Frankel, 'Migration and ethnicity in prehistoric Cyprus: technology as *habitus*'. *European Journal of Archaeology* 3 (2000) pp. 167–187.
Jennifer Webb and David Frankel, 'Characterising the Philia facies. Material culture, chronology and the origin of the Bronze Age in Cyprus'. *American Journal of Archaeology* 10 (1999) pp. 3–43.
Basil Hennessy, Kathryn Eriksson and Ina Kehrberg, *Ayia Paraskevi and Vasilia. Excavations by J.R.B. Stewart.* Studies in Mediterranean Archaeology LXXXII, Goteborg (1988).

7. Finding Marki
David Frankel and Jennifer Webb, *Marki Alonia. An Early and Middle Bronze Age Settlement in Cyprus.* Excavations 1995–2000. Studies in Mediterranean Archaeology CXXIII:2. Sävedalen (2006).
David Frankel and Jennifer Webb, 2008. *Marki. Life in a Cypriot Bronze Age Village.* Moufflon Publications, Nicosia (2008).
David Frankel and Jennifer Webb, 'Neighbours. Negotiating space in a prehistoric village'. *Antiquity* 80 (2006) pp. 287–302.
David Frankel and Jennifer Webb, 'Household continuity and transformation in a prehistoric Cypriot village'. In Bradley Parker and Catherine Foster (eds), *New Perspectives on Household Archaeology.* Eisenbrauns, Winona Lake (2012) pp. 473–500.

8. Observing crafty women

David Frankel and Jennifer Webb, *Marki Alonia. An Early and Middle Bronze Age Settlement in Cyprus. Excavations 1995–2000*. Studies in Mediterranean Archaeology CXXIII:2. Sävedalen (2006).

David Frankel and Jennifer Webb, 'Hobs and hearths in Bronze Age Cyprus'. *Opuscula Atheniensia* 20 (1994) pp. 51–56.

Vassos Karageorghis, *Aspects of Everyday Life in Ancient Cyprus: Inconographic Representations*. Leventis Foundation, Nicosia (2006).

Jennifer Webb and David Frankel, 'Hearth and home as identifiers of community in mid-third millennium Cyprus'. In Vassos Karageorghis and Ourania Kouka (eds), *On Cooking Pots, Drinking Cups, Loomweights and Ethnicity in Bronze Age Cyprus and Neighbouring Regions*. Leventis Foundation, Nicosia (2011) pp. 29–42.

Jennifer Webb and David Frankel, 'Prehistoric cooking pots from Cyprus'. *Ceramics Technical* 19 (2004) pp. 91–96.

Jennifer Webb, 'New evidence for the origins of textile production in Bronze Age Cyprus'. *Antiquity* 76 (2015) pp. 364-371.

9. Time and change

David Frankel, *Between the Murray and the Sea. Aboriginal Archaeology in Southeastern Australia*. Sydney University Press, Sydney (2017).

David Frankel, 'Characterising change in prehistoric sequences: a view from Australia'. *Archaeology in Oceania* 23 (1988) pp. 41–48.

Caroline Bird and David Frankel, *An Archaeology of Gariwerd. From Pleistocene to Holocene in Western Victoria*. Tempus 8. (Archaeology and Material Culture Studies in Anthropology) University of Queensland, St Lucia (2005).

Caroline Bird and David Frankel, 'Excavations at Koongine Cave: lithics and land use in the terminal Pleistocene and Holocene of South Australia'. *Proceedings of the Prehistoric Society* 67 (2001) pp. 49–83.

David Frankel, 'First-order radiocarbon dating of Australian shell-middens'. *Antiquity* 65 (1991) pp. 571–574.

David Frankel and Andrew Story, 'Dating shell middens – quickly and cheaply'. *Australian Aboriginal Studies* 1990/1 (1990) pp. 33–35.

Daniel Zobel, David Frankel and Ron Vanderwal, 'The Moonlight Head Rockshelter'. *Proceedings of the Royal Society of Victoria* 96 (1984) pp. 1–24.

David Frankel, 'Writing Aboriginal archaeology'. *Agora* 54.1 (2018) pp. 43–52.

David Frankel, David Thomas, Rebekah Kurpiel, Caroline Spry, Jacqui Tumney, Lorena Becerra-Valdivia and Bunurong Land Council Aboriginal Corporation, 'Late Holocene drying of Port Phillip Bay: Archaeological and cultural perspectives' *Australian Journal of*

Earth Sciences 70(6) (2023) pp. 890–897.

Guy Holdgate, Barbara Wagstaff, and Stephen. Gallagher, 'Did Port Phillip Bay nearly dry up between ~2800 and 1000 cal. yr BP? Bay floor channeling evidence, seismic and core dating' *Australian Journal of Earth Sciences* 58 (2011) pp. 157–175.

Carolyn Briggs, 'The filling of the bay – the time of chaos' (2023). https://victoriancollections.net.au/stories/nyernila---listen-continuously-aboriginal-creation-sto/metropolitan-and-central-victoria.

10. From one stone tool

David Frankel, *Between the Murray and the Sea. Aboriginal Archaeology in Southeastern Australia*. Sydney University Press, Sydney (2017).

Caroline Bird and David Frankel, 'Excavations at Koongine Cave: Lithics and land use in the terminal Pleistocene and Holocene of South Australia'. *Proceedings of the Prehistoric Society* 67 (2001) pp. 49–83.

11. Bull in a china shop

David Frankel and Jennifer Webb, 'A potter's workshop from Middle Bronze Age Cyprus: new light on production context, scale and variability'. *Antiquity* 88 (2014) pp. 425-440.

Jennifer Webb and David Frankel, *Ambelikou Aletri. Metallurgy and Pottery Production in Middle Bronze Age Cyprus*. Studies in Mediterranean Archaeology CXXXVIII, Uppsala (2013).

David Frankel, 'Recovering two ancient sites in Cyprus'. *Humanities Australia* 4 (2013) pp. 74–83.

12. A mild obsession

David Frankel, 'Illustration, allusion and commentary: Choosing the Four Sons in 1695'. *Images: A Journal of Jewish Art and Visual Culture* 4 (2010) pp. 18–24.

David Frankel, 'Romulus and Moses: expressing social conformity through images of the past in the Amsterdam Haggadot of 1695 and 1712'. *Australian Journal of Jewish Studies* 35 (2022) pp. 106–126.

13. You pays your money

Porphyrios Dikaios, *The Excavations at Vounous-Bellapais in Cyprus, 1931–2*. Archaeologia 88. The Society of Antiquaries of London, Oxford (1940).

Vassos Karageorghis, *The Coroplastic Art of Ancient Cyprus. I Chalcolithic – Late Cypriot I*. A.G. Leventis Foundation, Nicosia (1991).

David Frankel and Angela Tamvaki, 'Cypriot shrine models and decorated tomb facades'. *Australian Journal of Biblical Archaeology* 2.2 (1973) pp. 39–44.

Bernard Knapp, *Prehistoric and Protohistoric Cyprus: Identity, Insularity and Connectivity*. Oxford University Press, Oxford (2008).

14. Lime, chemistry and style

Giorgos Georgiou, Jennifer Webb and David Frankel, *Psematismenos Trelloukkas. An Early Bronze Age Cemetery in Cyprus*. Department of Antiquities, Cyprus, Nicosia (2011).

David Frankel and Jennifer Webb, 'Pottery production and distribution in prehistoric Bronze Age Cyprus. An application of pXRF analysis'. *Journal of Archaeological Science* 39 (2012) pp. 1380–1387.

Jennifer Webb and David Frankel, 'Cultural regionalism and divergent social trajectories in Early Bronze Age Cyprus'. *American Journal of Archaeology* 117.1 (2013) pp. 59–81.

David Frankel and Jennifer Webb, 'Colours and clouds of Bronze Age Cyprus'. *Ceramics Technical* 29 (2009) pp. 3–7.

15. Not Elizabeth's boot scraper

David Frankel, 'Excavations at Elizabeth Farm House, 1972'. *The Artefact* 4.3-4 (1979) pp. 39–56.

Kenneth Graham, *The Wind in the Willows* (1908).

16. Obsolescence

David Frankel, *Middle Cypriot White Painted Pottery: An Analytical Study of the Decoration*. Studies in Mediterranean Archaeology XLII, Göteborg (1974).

David Frankel, 'Inter site relationships in the Middle Bronze Age of Cyprus'. *World Archaeology* 6.2 (1974) pp. 190–208.

17. A menagerie

David Frankel, *Corpus of Cypriote Antiquities: 7. Early and Middle Bronze Age Material in the Ashmolean Museum, Oxford*. Studies in Mediterranean Archaeology XX:7, Göteborg (1983).

Ashmolean Museum, *Ashsmolean Museum, Oxford: Cyprus Collection*. https://www.ashmolean.org/cyprus.

18. Water monkeys and wine

Judy Birmingham, 'The archaeological contribution to nineteenth-century history: Some Australian case studies'. *World Archaeology* 7.3 (1976) pp. 306–317.

Anne Bickford and Associates, *The Irrawang Pottery Site. Assessment of Cultural Significance and Options for its Future. Final Report* (1993). https://digital.library.sydney.edu.au/nodes/view/9106.

Susan Lawrence and Peter Davies, *An Archaeology of Australia since 1788*. Springer, New York (2011).

Read more about it

19. Significance

David Frankel, *Between the Murray and the Sea. Aboriginal Archaeology in Southeastern Australia*. Sydney University Press, Sydney (2017).

David Frankel, *Remains to be Seen: Archaeological Insights into Australian Prehistory*. Longman Cheshire, Melbourne (1991).

David Frankel, 'Earth rings at Sunbury, Victoria'. *Archaeology in Oceania* 17.2 (1982) pp. 89–97.

David Frankel and Janine Major (eds), *Victorian Aboriginal Life and Customs through Early European Eyes*. La Trobe University EBureau, Melbourne (2017). https://library.latrobe.edu.au/ebureau/ebook.html#victorian.

Caroline Spry and 20 others, 'New braided knowledge understandings of an Aboriginal earth ring and *biik wurrdha* (Jacksons Creek, Sunbury) on Wurundjeri Woi-wurrung Country, southeastern Australia' *Australian Archaeology* 91 (2025).

20. By the numbers

David Frankel and Jennifer Webb, 'Population, households and ceramic consumption in a prehistoric Cypriot village'. *Journal of Field Archaeology* 28 (2001) pp. 115–129.

David Frankel and Jennifer Webb, 2006. *Marki Alonia. An Early and Middle Bronze Age Settlement in Cyprus. Excavations 1995–2000*. Studies in Mediterranean Archaeology CXXIII: 2. Sävedalen (2006).

George Eliot, *Silas Marner* (1861).

21. Recycling Sotira

Porphyrios Dikaios, *Sotira*. Philadelphia: University Museum, University of Pennsylvania (1961).

David Frankel, 'Constructing Sotira. Discard and deposition at a Neolithic village in Cyprus'. In Giorgos Vavouranakis and Ioannis Voskos (eds), *Metioessa, Studies in Honour of Eleni Mantzourani*. The Athens University Review of Archaeology (AURA) Supplement 10, Kardamitsa, Athens (2022) pp. 317–324.

Edgar Peltenburg, 'The Sotira Culture: Regional diversity and cultural unity in Late Neolithic Cyprus'. *Levant* 10 (1978) pp. 55–74.

Nicholas Stanley-Price, 'The structure of settlement at Sotira in Cyprus'. *Levant* 11 (1979) pp. 46–81.

22. Questioning mounds

Peter Beveridge, 'Of the Aborigines inhabiting the great lacustrine and Riverina depression of the lower Murray, lower Murrumbidgee, lower Lachlan, and lower Darling'. *Journal and Proceedings of the Royal Society of New South Wales* 17 (1883) pp. 19–74.

Annette Berryman and David Frankel, 'Archaeological investigations of mounds on the Wakool River, near Barham, New South Wales: a preliminary account'. *Australian Archaeology* 19 (1984) pp. 21–30.

Bill Downey and David Frankel, 'Radiocarbon and thermoluminescence dating of a Central Murray mound'. *The Artefact* 15 (1992) pp. 31–34.

David Frankel, *Remains to be Seen: Archaeological Insights into Australian Prehistory.* Longman Cheshire, Melbourne (1991).

David Frankel, *Between the Murray and the Sea. Aboriginal Archaeology in Southeastern Australia.* Sydney University Press, Sydney (2017).

Peter Coutts, Peter Henderson and Richard Fullagar. 'A preliminary investigation of Aboriginal mounds in northwestern Victoria'. *Records of the Victorian Archaeological Survey* 9 (1979).

23. Strike me pink

Jennifer Webb and David Frankel, 'Characterising the Philia facies. Material culture, chronology and the origin of the Bronze Age in Cyprus'. *American Journal of Archaeology* 103 (1999) pp. 3–43.

David Frankel and Jennifer Webb, *Marki Alonia. An Early and Middle Bronze Age Settlement in Cyprus. Excavations 1995–2000.* Studies in Mediterranean Archaeology CXXIII:2. Sävedalen (2006).

Maria Dikomitou-Eliadou, 'Rescaling perspective: local and island-wide ceramic production in Early and Middle Bronze Age Cyprus'. In Jennifer Webb (ed.), *Structure, Measurement and Meaning, Studies on Prehistoric Cyprus in Honour of David Frankel.* Studies in Mediterranean Archaeology CXLIII (2014) pp. 199—211.

David Frankel, 'Uniformity and variation in a Cypriot ceramic tradition'. *Levant* XII (1981) pp. 88–106.

David Frankel, 'Color variation on prehistoric Cypriot Red Polished Pottery'. *Journal of Field Archaeology* 21 (1994) pp. 205–219.

25. To see oursels

David Frankel, 'An active teaching museum at La Trobe University'. *Kalori* 58 (1980) pp. 3–6.

Caroline Bird and David Frankel, 'The university in the community: The Hamilton and Western District Museum'. *Conference of Museum Anthropologists Bulletin* 17 (1985) pp. 8–11.

26. Development

Jennifer Webb and David Frankel, 'Making an impression: storage and surplus finance in Late Bronze Age Cyprus'. *Journal of Mediterranean Archaeology* 7 (1994) pp. 5–27.

Joanna Smith, 'Theme and style in Cypriot wooden roller impressions'. *Cahiers du Centre d'Études Chypriotes* 37 (2007) pp. 347–374.

Read more about it

Bernard Knapp, *Prehistoric and Protohistoric Cyprus: Identity, Insularity and Connectivity.* Oxford University Press, Oxford (2008).

27. What you see is what you get

David Frankel, Denise Gaughwin, Caroline Bird and Roger Hall, 'Coastal archaeology in south Gippsland'. *Australian Archaeology* 28 (1989) pp. 14–25.

Joanna Fresløv and David Frankel, 'Abundant fields? A review of coastal archaeology in Victoria'. In Jay Hall and Ian McNiven (eds), *Australian Coastal Archaeology.* Research Papers in Archaeology and Natural History No. 31, Department of Prehistory, Research School of Pacific Studies, Australian National University, Canberra (1999) pp. 239–254.

David Frankel, *Between the Murray and the Sea. Aboriginal Archaeology in Southeastern Australia.* Sydney University Press, Sydney (2017).

28. Hunting a solution

Jennifer Webb, David Frankel, Paul Croft and Carole McCartney, 'Excavations at Politiko Kokkinorotsos: a Chalcolithic hunting station in Cyprus'. *Proceedings of the Prehistoric Society* 75 (2009) pp. 189–238.

David Frankel, 'A different Chalcolithic: A central Cypriot scene'. In Diane Bolger and Louise Maguire (eds), *The Development of Pre-State Communities in the Ancient Near East: Studies in Honour of Edgar Peltenburg.* Oxbow, Oxford (2010) pp. 38–45.

David Frankel, Jennifer Webb and Anne Pike-Tay, 'Seasonality and site function in Chalcolithic Cyprus'. *European Journal of Archaeology* 16 (2013) pp. 94–115.

Michael Given and Bernard Knapp, *The Sydney Cyprus Survey Project: Social Approaches to Regional Archaeological Survey.* Monumenta Archaeologica 21, The Cotsen Institute of Archaeology, University of California, Los Angeles (2003).

29. Back stories

Jennifer Webb and David Frankel, 'Characterising the Philia facies. Material culture, chronology and the origin of the Bronze Age in Cyprus'. *American Journal of Archaeology* 103 (1999) pp. 3–43.

David Frankel, 'Migration and ethnicity in prehistoric Cyprus: technology as habitus'. *European Journal of Archaeology* 3 (2000) pp. 167–187.

Jennifer Webb, *Exploring the Bronze Age in Cyprus. Australian Perspectives.* Fifth Maurice Kelly Lecture, Museum of Antiquities, University of New England (2002).

Einar Gjerstad, *Ages and Days in Cyprus*. Studies in Mediterranean Archaeology Pocketbook 12, Gothenburg (1980).

Judy Powell, *Love's Obsession. The Lives and Archaeology of Jim and Eve Stewart*. Wakefield Press, Kent Town (2013).

Porphyrios Dikaios and James Stewart, *The Stone Age and the Early Bronze Age in Cyprus*. The Swedish Cyprus Expedition Volume IV Part IA. Lund (1962).

30. Not an afterthought

Jean Kennedy, Chris Ballard and Stuart Bedford, 'Jack: Professor Jack Golson, AO, 1926–2023'. *Australian Archaeology* 89(3) (2023) pp. 275–277.

Jean Kennedy, Stuart Bedford, and Jim Allen, 'Experimental archaeologist, Wallace Raymond Ambrose 1933–2024'. *Australian Archaeology* 90(2) (2024) pp. 249–252.

Jack Golson, Jim Specht and Sharon Sullivan, 'Ronald John (Ron) Lampert (1927–2008)'. *Australian Academy of the Humanities Proceedings* 33 (2008) pp. 64–68. https://oa.anu.edu.au/obituary/lampert-ronald-john-ron-32742.

Stephen Bourke. 'J. Basil Hennessy AO (1925–2013)'. *Levant* 46 (2014) pp. 1–3,

Basil Hennessy, 'In Memoriam: Anthony Walter McNicoll'. *Bulletin of the American Schools of Oriental Research* 265 (1987) pp. 1–2.

Tracy Ireland and Mary Casey, 'Judy Birmingham in conversation'. *Australasian Historical Archaeology* 24 (2006) pp. 7–16.

David Frankel, 'Judy Birmingham: impressions and influences'. https://www.awaws.org/history-of-women/judy-birmingham-impressions-and-influences.

The illustrations: notes and credits

ii	Frontispiece cartoon by Michael Pickering
viii	Lena, on a visit to ancient sites at Arad, January 1968
ix	Map of Cyprus showing main places referred to in these stories
x	Maps of Australia and Papua New Guinea showing main places referred to in these stories
1	The 'White Obelisk' of Ashurnasirpal in the British Museum (© The Trustees of the British Museum)
3	Entrance shafts to two tombs at Deneia
4	A looted tomb used as a rubbish dump
5	Plotting the location of tombs with a high-precision GPS, 2003; An exhausted Rudy Frank; A plan showing the location of visible tomb entrances in one area near Deneia Village
6	A large shed once used as a pottery factory which became the expedition storage and workspace; Entrance shaft of a looted tomb with a large stone slab which originally closed off the entrance to the chamber below; Students working underground; Sieving excavated soil to find small bones and artefacts
7	Mending and studying the thousands of fragments collected from looted tombs at Deneia
9	'The warriors of Urama' – a Long House in Kinomere Village, photographed by Frank Hurley, 1921; The newly built Long House in 1981
10	Tidal swamps of the Kikori Delta; Canoes provide the only way to travel through these waterways; Loading a *lagatoi* trading canoe at Port Morseby. Photograph by J.W. Lindt in the 1880s (State Library of Victoria, La Trobe Picture Collection); Excavating fragments of pottery from sites in the Papuan Gulf
11	Excavating in the centre of Kinomere Village, 1981; Local children 'helping'

The illustrations: notes and credits

13 James Stewart on a donkey; View down to the north coast of Cyprus from the excavations at Karmi, 1961

14 Eve Stewart drawing a plan of a tomb at Karmi (Photo: Robert Merrillees

15 Carvings on the side wall of Karmi Palealona Tomb 6

16 The 'Tomb of the Seafarer' (Karmi Palealona Tomb 11B): photo and plan; the Middle Cypriot I White Painted Ware II jug and the Cretan Middle Minoan Kamares Ware cup

17 Raquel Welch at Karmi in 1970 with a group of local women

19 Morovi Iuaia of Kinomere Village with a half-finished Gope Board; 'The Gope of a Urama shrine' – an array of boards and pig skulls in the Long House at Kinomere Village, photographed by Frank Hurley, 1923

20 'The interior of the great Dubu Daima of Urama' – inside the Long House at Kinomere Village, photographed by Frank Hurley, 1921

21 The craftsman at work: stages in the carving of a Gope board

22 Pigments and painting the completed carving

23 Metal sample No. 5; Axe UNEMA 74/6/3 from Vasilia from which it was taken

24 Metalwork in the University of New England Museum of Antiquities sampled for compositional analysis

26 Cache of metal items uncovered by J.R. Stewart in the entrance to Vasilia Tomb 1 (Photo: Eve Stewart and Basil Hennessy); Artefacts probably from Vasilia bought by the Cyprus Museum in 1959 (Photograph with the permission of the Director of the Department of Antiquities, Cyprus)

29 Excavations in progress at Marki, 1998

30 Documenting and drawing pottery

32 Peter Davies describing and drawing three superimposed walls; Delese Brewster documenting a plaster hearth surround in Unit CII

33 The plaster hearth on the left replaced an earlier one, the remains of which are just visible showing through the floor on the right; Walls and features of different Phases of construction in Unit CXXI

The illustrations: notes and credits

34　A page of an excavation logbook

35　A schematic diagram of the sequence of deposits, walls and features in Unit CII and three adjacent Units

36　Plans of four of the main Phases of development at Marki. The colours identify household compounds (darker shades are interior rooms, lighter shades are courtyards). Grey indicates access lanes and white open spaces and ruins; Imaginative reconstructions by Alexander Perrin of the excavated area of Marki in Phases B, E, G and H (people and goats not shown)

39　Photograph and formal drawing of pottery spindle whorl P8422 from Marki

40　Could a Bronze Age spinner have looked like this?; Heavy clay weights for use with a warp-weighted loom; Copper needles

41　Perhaps the decoration on this 'plank figurine' represents ornaments and decoration on a Bronze Age Cypriot woman's dress; Penny Maroulis finding a well-used heavy stone rubber; upper rubber and lower quern used for grinding wheat and barley

42　We were very puzzled when we found our first fragmentary hob as we'd never seen anything like it before

43　Reconstructed hob; Cooking pot; Excavating burial jar P14040 at Marki

44　Model of a woman with her baby in a cradle-board, Lapithos Tomb 307B.13 (Photograph with the permission of the Director of the Department of Antiquities, Cyprus)

46　Victoria Archaeological Survey excavations at Billimina (courtesy First Peoples–State Relations)

47　Left: Gariwerd today is heavily vegetated. Right: As it might have looked at the height of the last Ice Age, 18,000 years ago; Drawing of the side of the excavations at Koongine Cave showing deposits accumulated over less than 2,000 years from about 12,000 years ago (see the photo on p. 58)

49　Relative numbers of coastal shell middens through time along the western Victorian coast; A badly degraded, older midden on the coast of South-East South Australia

50　800 years of accumulated shells in the Moonlight Head midden

The illustrations: notes and credits

51 Two ways of seeing the evidence of shellfish collection at Moonlight Head: a. the sequence divided into four 200-year-long periods; b. divided into 27 far shorter periods

52 Collecting strategies through time at Moonlight Head seen as independent events, perhaps each a generation apart

53 Map of Port Phillip Bay (Naarm) today and as it was before 2,800 years ago; The same area between 2,800 and 1,000 years ago

55 Ken Mulvaney excavating Square J9 in Koongine Cave, 1982; 26/97, a 10,000-year old flint scraper that he found

56 Veins of flint in the limestone walls of Koongine Cave; The entrance to Gran Gran Cave, a source of fine quality flint; Tool marks from flint mining on the walls of Karlie-ngoinpool Cave (Photo: Robert Bednarik)

57 Markings scratched into the soft limestone wall of Koongine Cave

58 Excavations at Koongine Cave, 1982; Deposits accumulated over less than 2,000 years from about 12,000 years ago; A 'Gambieran' scraper exposed on the surface in the Kongorong Hills, South Australia

60 Excavations at Wyrie Swamp (Photo: Roger Luebbers); wooden spear and boomerang from Wyrie Swamp, now in the South Australian Museum

62 Caves in the limestone ridge overlooking low-lying wetlands

64 Mount Schank last erupted about 5,000 years ago

65 The entrance to the Cyprus Museum; Figures from Iron Age Ayia Irini

66 At work in the corridor between rows of storage cabinets; Trays of sherds and mended vessels from Ambelikou; Jenny Webb documenting pottery

67 Rudy Frank, Kathryn Eriksson and Wei Ming drawing and photographing pottery from Ambelikou in the Cyprus Museum

The illustrations: notes and credits

68 Two views of the jugs and other features on the floor of the potters' workshop at Ambelikou; Photo of the excavations used in the *Illustrated London News* of 2 March 1946 showing 'the kiln at right corner' (Photographs with the permission of the Director of the Department of Antiquities, Cyprus)

69 Plan of the pottery workshop showing the location of features, equipment and the jugs scattered across the floor; Imaginative reconstruction by Alexander Perrin of what the interior of the potters' workshop may have looked like, although it was probably never so clean and tidy

71 Ten of the 39 jugs from the workshop at Ambelikou

73 The 'Four Sons' as engraved for the 1695 Amsterdam *Haggadah* by Abraham ben Jacob

74 Title page of the 1695 Amsterdam *Haggadah*

75 Matthaus Merian the Elder; Entry on Abraham ben Jacob in Johan Wolf's *Bibliotheca Hebraea* (1727)

76 Herodotus in Athens with the young Thucydides beside him (Matthaus Merian, Gottfried's *Historische Chronik*, 1619)

77 Young Hannibal swearing enmity to Rome (Matthaus Merian, Gottfried's *Historische Chronik*, 1619); Saul being given directions by Samuel (Matthaus Merian, *Icones Biblicae*, 1630)

78 Assyrian army fleeing from Jerusalem (Matthaus Merian, *Icones Biblicae,* 1630)

79-80 The 'Vounous model' as restored from fragments excavated by Porphyrios Dikaios from Bellapais Vounous Tomb 22 (Photographs with the permission of the Director of the Department of Antiquities, Cyprus)

83 Entrance shaft to an Early Bronze Age tomb at Psematismenos revealed as a bulldozer carefully scrapes away the limestone overburden; Cyprus Department of Antiquities excavators hard at work; pottery revealed in a small underground tomb chamber (Photographs with the permission of the Director of the Department of Antiquities, Cyprus)

The illustrations: notes and credits

84 Excavating a small tomb chamber; Removing encrusted limestone deposits; Documenting pottery from Psematismenos at the Larnaca Museum

85 Using a portable XRF analyser to assess quantities of trace elements in the clay of a bowl

86 Principal Components Analysis of trace elements in the clays of vessels from Psematismenos (green) and Bellapais Vounous (red); Two small bowls from Bellapais Vounous on the north coast of Cyprus which have the same chemical signature as those from the south coast

87 Two Early Bronze Age vessels from Bellapais Vounous with characteristic formally structured incised decoration; Four Early Bronze Age bowls from Psematismenos with typically random but deliberate mottling of the surface;

88 Two Middle Bronze Age vessels from Deneia; Diversity of incised patterns on fragments of bowls from Deneia

91 A boot-scraper beside the entrance to Elizabeth Farm House; Excavations in progress, 1972

92 The sequence of layers beside the front verandah – note the grey-filled wheel-rut in the white gravel (below the back-and-white scale); Excavations across the front lawn

93 Older bearers showing the location of earlier, demolished parts of the building; Post-holes which once supported a light structure beside the main building; The original cellar below the entrance hall; Clay pipe fragments and an 1816 coin

94 The New South Wales Institution for the Deaf, Dumb and Blind (Mitchell Library, State Library of New South Wales); Old and new incarnations of Elizabeth Farm House

95 Documenting Middle Bronze Age pottery in the Cyprus Museum, 1971

96 A sample of Middle Bronze Age White Painted Ware; IBM computer card punch; A stack of punch cards (https://www.ibm.com/history/punched-card)

97 Cluster analysis grouping sets of pots on the basis of their shared designs and the main groups plotted on a map of Cyprus

The illustrations: notes and credits

99 Small Bronze Age Cypriot bottle C361 in the British Museum; Some Bronze Age people and animals in the Ashmolean Museum, Oxford

100 Photo, original drawing and inked final copy of a jug and its place among friends on a page of the *Corpus of Early and Middle Bronze Age Material in the Ashmolean Museum*

103 Identifying stamp on a pottery fragment from Irrawang; Working and camping during first seasons of excavations at Irrawang, 1975

104 Examples of Irawang pottery and an advertisement from the *Sydney Morning Herald,* 22 December 1845; 'Irrawang Vineyard and Pottery', engraving by John Carmichael, 1838

105 Peter Callaghan and Meg Smee excavating at Irrawang

106 The excavated remains of mills for processing clay and one of the kilns at Irrawang; Fragments of decorated pottery

107 Relaxing after a hard day excavating at Irrawang

109 The earth ring in the Mumilan Korobine Nature Reserve, Sunbury, before it was swamped by housing development; Dan Witter at an earth ring at Rupertswood, Sunbury, 1978

110 Volunteer Regiment at Sunbury, 1867 (Engraving by Edmond Goss); Excavating one earth ring at Sunbury, 1978; The stone cairn in the centre of the excavated ring

113 Wurundjeri Woi-wurrung Elder Allan Wandin examining chipped stone artefacts from Sunbury in the Museum Victoria storeooms in 2022; Wurundjeri Woi-wurrung Elder Ron Jones at Sunbury

115 Washing thousands of pottery sherds, always a tedious task; Jenny Webb documenting pottery from Marki

116 Tim Hill mending pots and a sample of his completed work

118 Pieces of a bowl with mend holes

119 Porphyrios Dikaios, about the time when he first found the site at Sotira; The Sotira Teppes hill; Neolithic wall footings conserved on the site

121 A plan of the main excavation area at Sotira showing walls of different Phases

181

The illustrations: notes and credits

123 Relative proportions of the two main pottery wares in each Phase at Sotira

125 Looking at a mound beside the Wakool River

127 Roger Hall plotting the location of mounds on an air photo; Measuring a low mound; Distribution of mounds; Relationship between mound size and nearest water body.

129 Baked clay heat-retainers raked out of an earth oven; A mound rises above flood waters; Tree with a scar left by the removal of bark to make a canoe

132 Munsell soil colour chart for Hue 2.5YR; Recording colour and other attributes of excavated sherds

133 Red Polished (Philia) sherds; Early Red Polished sherds; Distribution of surface colours of Red Polished and Red Polished (Philia) wares

134 Distribution of fabric colours of Red Polished and Red Polished (Philia) wares

135 Relative proportions of different grades of fabric hardness of Red Polished and Red Polished (Philia) wares

137 Kostis G. Polystipiotis Kitchenware Shop today, now run by our Mr Polystipiotis' son https://lh3.googleusercontent.com/p/AF1QipOz5aB-eW7OazRq_q2JAKfc-4yYwwCKHoDSwAhA=s680-w680-h510.

139 Setting up museum displays in the La Trobe University Prehistory and Anthropology Museum

141 Jenny Webb documenting artefacts at Analiondas Palioklichia, 1992

142 Distribution of pithos sherds and stone artefacts at Palioklichia; Rolled impression on a pithos sherd

144 Agricultural development transforming the landscape at Analiondas

145 Gideon, Lena and Daniel at our house on Cassia Street, Cape Paterson in 1985; Students finding a midden exposed in the dunes; Denise Gaughwin explaining something to Joanna Fresløv (and her baby David) on the dune overlooking the mouth of the Powlett River

146 Beaches and cliffs at Cape Paterson; Recording eroding shell middens

147	Some of the main rock-platform species of shellfish found on the Victorian coast
148	Caroline Bird recording stone artefacts on an eroded section of the dunes
149	Politiko Kokkinorotsos, 2008
150	Hollows and pits in the excavated area at Kokkinorotsos
151	Excavating at Politiko Kokkinorotsos; Processing finds in 2008
152	Examples of chipped stone tools from Kokkinorotsos
153	Paul Croft examining animal bones
154	Mandibles sampled for teeth of fallow deer (above) and moufflon (below); Time range when each animal sampled was killed
155	Paul Åström; Eve and Jim Stewart
156	Porphyrios Dikaios
157	Members of the Swedish Cyprus Expedition in 1930 – John Lindros, Alfred Westholm, Erik Sjöqvist and Einar Gjerstad
159	My well-worn copy of SCE IV 1A
163	Jack Golson and Wal Ambrose in the rain at the Maori pā (hill-fort) at Kauri Point, New Zealand (1967); Ron Lampert at the Burrill Lake rockshelter, NSW (1968); Judy Birminham at the Geometric Period town at Zagora, Greece (1969), Tony McNicholl and Basil Hennessy at Chalcolithic Teleilat Ghassul, Jordan (1977)
185	In the Larnaca Museum, 2008 (Photo by Peter Saad)

David Frankel studied archaeology at the University of Sydney before going on to complete a PhD at Gothenburg University, Sweden. After some years at The British Museum, he returned to Australia in 1978 to take up a lectureship at La Trobe University in Melbourne. Retiring after 35 years, as an Emeritus Professor he maintains a close connection with the Department of Archaeology and History at the university.

He is Joint Editor of the Swedish monograph series Studies in Mediterranean Archaeology, a Fellow of the Australian Academy of the Humanities and a Member of the Australian Institute of Aboriginal and Torres Strait Islander Studies. In 2015 he was awarded the Rhys Jones Medal for Outstanding Contributions to Australian Archaeology by the Australian Archaeological Association.

His primary research interests are in Australian Aboriginal archaeology and in the archaeology of Bronze Age Cyprus. He has directed excavations at a range of sites in Australia, Cyprus and Papua New Guinea, many of which provide the basis for these stories. His recent general books include *Between the Murray and the Sea: Aboriginal Archaeology in Southeastern Australia* (2017), *Victorian Aboriginal Life and Customs through Early European Eyes* (2017) and a book for primary age children, *Digging up a Village: A Book about Archaeology* (2019).

David lives in Melbourne with his wife Lena (to say nothing of the dog), not far from their two sons and three grandchildren.

Archaeological incidents and accidents

Did you ever want to know about the reality of archaeological research? Try this. It might not satisfy a passion for temples, palaces and treasures of the rich and famous, or give you grand explanations of history. Instead you will find stories of everyday things and people encountered during a lifetime of work in Australia, Cyprus and Papua New Guinea. Always challenging, archaeology is serious business. But we should never take ourselves too seriously. These stories don't. Some are longer, some shorter and a few taller. There may be more questions than answers, as research may take unexpected directions, sometimes affected by unpredictable accidents, incidents and events. Things don't always go to plan.

David Frankel is an Emeritus Professor of Archaeology at La Trobe University in Melbourne.

www.ingramcontent.com/pod-product-compliance
Lightning Source LLC
LaVergne TN
LVHW070825250326
834741LV00033B/199